D1494121

KA 0351365 3

People's Pornography

For the rare birds, with deep respect for their babbling minds

People's Pornography

Sex and Surveillance on the Chinese Internet

Katrien Jacobs

intellect Bristol, UK / Chicago, USA

UNIVERSITY OF WINCHESTER
LIBRARY

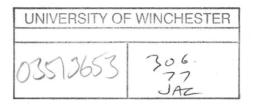

UNIVERSITY OF WINCHESTER

03512653 | 306.
77
JAZ

First published in the UK in 2012 by
Intellect, The Mill, Parnall Road, Fishponds, Bristol, BS16 3JG, UK

First published in the USA in 2012 by
Intellect, The University of Chicago Press, 1427 E. 60th Street,
Chicago, IL 60637, USA

Copyright © 2012 Intellect Ltd

All rights reserved. No part of this publication may be reproduced,
stored in a retrieval system, or transmitted, in any form or by
any means, electronic, mechanical, photocopying, recording, or
otherwise, without written permission.

A catalogue record for this book is available from the
British Library.

Cover designer: Holly Rose
Copy-editor: Heather Owen
Typesetting: Mac Style, Beverley, E. Yorkshire

ISBN 978-1-84150-493-3

Printed and bound by Hobbs, UK.

Contents

Acknowledgements

I knew from the onset that I was embarking on sensitive and censored topics, and it was a great relief to feel the love and support of so many individuals. First of all, I would like to thank all of you (and there are quite a few) who wish to remain anonymous. I also want to mention the writers and administrators of provocative web sites such as China Digital Times and China Media Project; and the many micro-bloggers on Twitter, who have kept their daily wits about Chinese Internet politics. Their statements and ways of sharing information, as well as their warmth, humor and resistance were crucial ingredients in researching and writing this book.

The research was partially funded by two Strategic Research Grants issued by City University of Hong Kong and by two General Research Funds issued by the University Grants Committee of the Hong Kong Special Administrative Region. I am indebted to several colleagues at Chinese University of Hong Kong for supporting my work and research. Thank You Lai Chi Tim, Laikwan Pang, Angela Wong, James Steintrager and Rochelle Yang in the department of Cultural and Religious Studies for your trust and feedback. Special thanks also to my colleagues at City University of Hong Kong – Anne Peirson-Smith for collaborating on the research about animation fandom and costume play, and for co-organizing the event *Extra/Ordinary Dresscode: Costuming and the Second Skin in Asia* (Hong Kong 2009). I am also indebted to Wan-Ying Lin and Mike Yao at City University for collaborating on the third chapter about pornography and gender. I would generally like to thank the Department of Media and Communication at City University of Hong Kong for encouraging my research, for generously funding all my travels to China and for allowing me to attend to several international conferences and arts festivals. Furthermore, I would also like to thank Helena Tsang and Joanne Tsang at the Research Grants office at City University of Hong Kong and the Chinese University of Hong Kong respectively, for their professional and wonderful attitude and helping me out with managing these grants, for making it not only a realistic goal but also a pleasant experience to apply for grant money.

I also would like to thank all the people who agreed to be speak openly for this book. Many of my students decided to participate in interviews and offered me their support in other ways. They were the positive force that kept me going in times of doubt and/or trouble. Then there were local Hong Kong scholars, friends, artists and activists who helped me argue against general repression and for sexual pleasures: Isaac Leung, Alvis Choi, Ellen Pau, Li Yinhe, Josephine Ho, John Erni, Gerrie Lim, Gina Marchetti, Helen Grace, Yau Ching, Denise Tang, Yvonne Lau, Oiwan Lam, Verdy Leung, and Siu Ding.

Many dedicated research assistants have over the years helped me search for materials, translate documents and transcribe interviews between three different languages – Mandarin, Cantonese, and English. Many others have acted as cultural mediators and have agreed to do simultaneous translations while interviewing people. Most of the research came out of an intricate process of intense collaborations over an extended period of time, which required a special kind of care for the project itself. I would like to thank Yan Liu, Nicola Tsang, Chengcai Yi, Firenze Lu and Jack Liu for connecting me with friends and for providing translations. Special thanks to Martin Sposato and Bing Czeng for helping me loosen up as a researcher. Thanks to Carrie Yang for working and thinking with me very closely in digging up and translating the raw materials about sex bloggers.

There were several scholars and curators who invited me to present parts of this book as work-in-progress, Tran T. Kim-Trang, Jurgen Bruenig, Tim Stuttgen, Johannes Grenzfurthner, Alessandro Ludovico and Mireille Miller-Young. Their help was invaluable in testing the waters and pulling me out of self-absorbedness. Thanks also to my network of "porn friends" for keeping in touch for all those years: Warbear, Sergio Messina, Susanna Passonen, Shu Lea Cheang, Matteo Pasquinelli, Fiona Attwood, Clarissa Smith, Ismail Necmi, Nat Muller, Tobaron Waxman, Chantal Zakari, Barbara de Genevieve, and many others.

The cover photograph was taken by Martin Lui and depicts the artist Siu Ding.

I wish to thank Intellect Books for their undivided interest and support and special thanks to Tim Mitchell for coordinating and materializing the project.

And finally, my deepest love to my husband Andrew Guthrie for proofreading the entire manuscript twice and for 24/7 feedback and support.

Introduction

This was a key invention of Mao's – to involve the entire population in the machinery of control. Few wrongdoers, according to the regime's criteria, could escape the watchful eyes of the people, especially in a society with an age-old concierge mentality.

Jung Chang, Wild Swans: Three Daughters of China

Citizens have the right of ownership of their bodies. They can use it and dispose of it as they want.

Dr. Li Yinhe

This book looks at how Chinese people use pornography and create online sexual identities to experience simple pleasures and to enter a more thorny quest for civil liberties. It also shows how Chinese governments are responding in a paradoxical manner – by denouncing pleasure industries while cultivating them as an area of capitalist expansion. The research for this book came out of my experiences of living and working in Hong Kong, which is a Special Administrative Region of the People's Republic of China and is geographically located at its South Eastern border. It has an autonomous political and legal system and makes for an ideal hub from which to travel around the region and carry out research into the Internet's effect on Chinese sexual pleasures. Hong Kong is also an ideal place to probe into attitudes towards pornography and surveillance culture, as citizens and researchers are by law protected under post-handover free-speech statutes, allowing them to browse and analyze sexually-explicit materials. The Internet itself is uncensored while topics of activism and sexual indiscretions are more-or-less-freely discussed amongst scholars and students.

Mainland web culture is different as all pornography sites and many foreign news sites or social networks are officially banned, even though some of these bans are at times lifted. As a result of erratic bouts of censorship and crackdowns on dissidents, such as the April 2011 detainment of celebrity artist Ai Wei Wei, mainland netizens have become at once savvy and cynical about open Internet culture and larger political changes. When talking about pornography and online sexuality as politically-vitalizing forces, Chinese citizens have a lot at stake, but these topics are sensitive and are very carefully monitored by government. Moreover, since so little research is being done about pornography in China in general, I have taken the opportunity to explore emerging porn culture and porn taste as an aspect of civil sexual emancipation.

Hong Kong's Internet culture is somewhat less flamboyant and fierce than the mainland's but it is, in fact, otherwise supported by excellent scholarly infrastructures and state-endorsed funding schemes. Through various research and arts grants, I was able to collaborate with Cantonese- and Mandarin-speaking research assistants in conducting fieldwork in Hong Kong, Taiwan, and China. I worked closely with my team in browsing web sites, searching for raw materials and conducting interviews with people who utilize and interact with sexually explicit materials. It was sometimes difficult to gather these materials and to interview people. When working in mainland China, given its draconian methods of enforcing "social stability," it was hard not to feel paranoid when dealing openly with these sensitive topics. I checked with scholars and students to find out what would be a potential, if not safe route of

Figure 1: Hong Kong woman wearing Ai Wei Wei mask to protest the April 2011 detainment of Chinese celebrity artist Ai Wei Wei. Photograph by Andrew Guthrie.

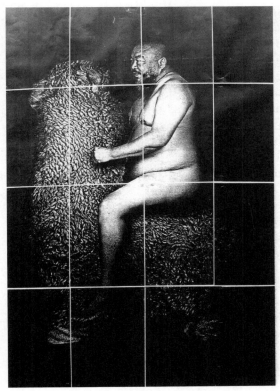

Figure 2: Protest Poster in defense of Ai Wei Wei made by students at City University of Hong Kong April 2011. The poster depicts the artist sitting on the "Grass Mud Horse," (草泥馬) the mythic animal that became an Internet meme in 2009 and was used widely to criticize censorship and defend the life of online obscenities. Photograph by Bing Czeng.

investigation. I received almost unanimous feedback that pornography was a "safe enough" topic, perhaps even a loophole in a system of tight control over individuals and sexual liberation. Reactions to my project in mainland China were overwhelmingly positive, but I was always glad to be able to withdraw to my safer space of play and reflection – Hong Kong.

Sex and pornography have become central forces in China's twenty-first-century politics, in its technology and cultural policies and in its blueprints for Internet governance. This book is a Chinese contribution to global pornography debates, which focuses on the attitudes and voices of Chinese (young) adults and the new generation of netizens, and their discussions of aesthetics, taste and pleasure. Beyond or attendant to a uniquely-Chinese perspective on taste, the analysis will be useful in imagining a global future for porn taste and surveillance culture. The book, therefore, is not founded in Western pornography scholarship, but tries to take media theory and civil rights debates beyond a dominant fascination with Western taste in film industries and digital networks.

The Chinese Communist Party aspires to control activism and political movements, yet it also promotes a specific type of netizen activity through commodity fetishism and/or consumerism. As Lisa Rofel (2007) has shown in her book *Desiring China: Experiments in Neoliberalism, Sexuality, and Public culture*, sexuality has become part of the ongoing negotiations about what it means to be a Chinese cosmopolitan citizen and a benign consumer (無害的消費者). Unlike the older generations, who were taught to accept political hardship and poverty, and the imposed abstinence of the Mao years, the younger generations are encouraged to free themselves of these lifestyle constraints. Their experimentation with sexually explicit media is somewhat encouraged if it is used towards a cosmopolitanism with Chinese characteristics (有中國特色的世界主義). These lifestyles are proudly or excessively materialistic, involving a soothing or quenching of "the dangerous passions of politics." Sex entertainment is a fashion to transcend restrictive local lifestyles but ultimately aims at a kind of patriotism or a social configuration of China's place in the world (Rofel 2007: 121).

Chinese citizens are encouraged to become part of a "New World Dream" (新世界梦想), which has been described in government propaganda as one that situates life within a harmonized "world city." Brian Holmes has observed how this mythic city is portrayed in terms of endless construction and expansion:

> … continuous buildings, endless highways, infinite urbanization, a city beyond the limits of the imagination. Huge urban blocks, surging arteries, expanding ring roads, metros, airports, refineries, power plants, bullet trains, a city that devours the countryside, scraping the mountains and the sky. (Holmes 2008).

The process of entering the world city is often described in Chinese as "jumping in the sea" (下海), an expression that indicates the way that people are forced to leave behind the old securities of communist living and begin to conduct themselves as entrepreneurial risk-takers. As Holmes concludes, the Chinese government has developed a unique if not awkward balance between a normative or repressive political system and wildly-expansive economy of goods and services. This has created a paradoxical sense of openness surrounding the consumerist-oriented youth and sex cultures. China's famous rock star, Cui Jian, or "Old Cui" (老崔) as he is called, elegantly mirrors this point in an interview: "Politics are simply too dangerous. It tears into your soul and ruins your life" (Williams 1997).

Even though the sexual indiscretions portrayed in this book are uniquely Chinese, they also typify a future for global sex culture as they are driven by global corporate ownership and attitudes of benign consumerism or public acquiescence. Mimi Sheller has developed a "mobilities theory" in order to rethink the study of modern cultures impacted by the global infrastructures of neo-liberalism. Sheller's work analyzes the impact of virtual tourism in the Caribbean region, showing how IT corporations and creative industries are imposing global imaginaries of upward mobility and commerce. These sites of alluring and soothing virtuality create novel lifestyles and work opportunities for the local population, but also produce obvious sites of destitution and lethargy. (Sheller 2007: 18) Similarly, as a result of a new kind of sexual virtuality that affects Chinese cities and even rural localities, people are increasingly partaking in transnational networks for personal matters of romance and sex work. People almost organically project their bodies and minds into global domains and networks, yet they have to hide these impulses when dealing with traditional forms of government and/or family planning. A paradoxical ethos of pleasure and depression/ denial controls the growth of sex industries, with more room for satisfaction and hypocrisy amongst privileged classes. Besides arguing for the acceptance and democratization of porn industries and sex entertainment, the book reveals the underground cultures of art and activist disobedience, those who show strength, humor and difference within the wasteland of Chinese pornography education.

One famous case of the political persecution of a sex radical that took place in mainland China in 2010 was that of Professor Ma Xiaohai of Nanjing (南京某大學教授马晓海). Professor Ma was sentenced to three-and-a-half years in prison for "crowd licentiousness" after he engaged in casual group sex as a swinger. Even though hundreds of thousands of Chinese people are trying out similar lifestyles through online hook-up platforms, there are ancient Chinese obscenity laws against multi-partner sex or "hooliganism." Professor Ma would have been free to pursue his passions in most other nation states, and he spoke eloquently and confidently about casual sex in various statements, but few Chinese public commentators defended or stood up for him when he received an excessive jail sentence (Wong 2010). Mainland academia is perhaps overtly associated with values of state-enforced intellectual responsibility and bodily denial and, hence, would foster little public support for an academic "sex machine" such as Professor Ma.

One exception in this pattern of complacency or fear of difference is by one of China's leading sexologist, Dr. Yinhe of the Beijing Academy of Social Sciences (北京社科院李銀河博士), who defended Professor Ma as a progressive thinker and activist in defense of sexual minorities. She argued that Professor Ma was wrongly accused as there were no victims involved and the sex acts took place in a private space amongst consenting adults. Most cases of "crowd licentiousness" (swinging, orgies, etc.) have been dropped in China, indicating that the Nanjing police force must be extremely conservative. Dr. Li Yinhe added that the media buzz around Professor Ma shows that China was opening up to alternative lifestyles. As she stated in a video interview on joy.cn:

> I do not agree with swinging, neither do I like it. But if consenting couples want to do it because of aesthetic fatigue, they bring no harm to the society or to themselves. To my knowledge, couples who practice swinging enjoy better marital relationships than general couples. Only couples who are really intimate can communicate this well and not be jealous about it. It's a feature of the swingers. They are doing it because they are curious or they like it this way. I defend the right of minorities. (Li 2010)

The Chinese Internet has made for a broader space for unorthodox lifestyles and social discourses. While ancient obscenity laws are still in place and are occasionally applied to persecute sex radicals or porn distributors, Chinese netizens are nevertheless engaged in a kind of revolt (Hu 2009: 16). As will be shown in the analysis of activism and blogging discourses, sexuality constitutes a powerful "animal force" as netizens seize the opportunity to and take part in pornography's inter-connected political debates.

But at the same time, the force of governmental interference and anti-obscenity campaigns culminated in mainland China in 2009, when seven different government agencies collaborated and issued a televised report concerning the "Anti-Vulgarity Political Campaign" (反三俗政治運動) In Fall 2010, it was reported that 1,332 Chinese citizens had been convicted by the Supreme People's Court for "spreading pornography" through the internet and text messages. Fifty-eight of those convicted had been jailed for five years or more and the youngest person convicted was 19 years old. (South China Morning Post [SCMP] 2010)

Several commentators adopted the term of "Confucian Confusion" to describe the discrepancy between the government's sex-phobic morality and the commercially-sponsored or citizen-driven networks for sexual entertainment. It took me some time to wrap my head around this "CC" but I eventually realized that I had to exploit it as a crack within the system. Neither antiquated phobias nor sexual freedom can stand alone in this circumstance, but will exemplify the quarreling and discordant forces in contemporary Chinese society. As argued by Feng Chien-san (馮建三) in *Info Rhizome,* it is vital for scholars to make use of these internal quarrels within the state apparatus: "There are countless reasons for internal conflicts taking place within the state apparatus, and it is up to us to punch our needles into the fissures whenever they appear" (Feng 2009: 18).

Let us further probe this "porn crack" by means of an anecdote. Towards the end of my writing process, an informant sent me more evidence that Chinese netizens are sharing sexually explicit materials on peer-to-peer file-sharing sites hosted on overseas servers. Then he added that the "porn sites" that Chinese netizens are most frequently using are those that are actually linked to banned news items. So the circulation of sexually explicit media is somewhat safer than the banned news about political topics. In formulating this unique coalescence of sexual and political curiosity, my book is indebted to Matteo Pasquinelli, who has helped me formulate a critical yet sex-positive perspective on emerging netporn cultures (色情文化振興). In his book *Animal Spirits: A Bestiary of the Commons,* Pasquinelli looks at different mythical animals and how they might constitute useful symbols for conceptualizing power within new media culture. Just as political leaders and CEO's of world-class institutions can appropriate lions, snakes and dragons as emblems of power, media artists can reclaim mythical creatures, and their animalistic power instincts (Pasquinelli 2009). This perspective is valuable in coming to an understanding of erotic activism in mainland China where one such humorous symbol of sexual rebellion is the "Grass Mud Horse" (草泥马), which was invented to collectively criticize government propaganda. The Grass Mud Horse is one of twelve fictional creatures that were invented on the web-based encyclopedia Baidu Baike (百度百科) and whose names closely resemble profanities in the Chinese language. Even though the surreal animal-figures and their associated mythologies were officially banned in 2009, they had already conquered the Internet and were circulated by those in favor of open Internet culture and sexual entertainment.

Erotic energy and a collective sense of humor have helped netizens to keep up with a joyful variety of activism, one where contentious identities can be developed and indulged. The ability to escape from restrictive cultural attitudes through Internet culture and to question the immense pressures of a national surveillance culture constitutes a sense of freedom and vitality. These types of freedom provide entertainment and relief but do not entail a deeper disruption of power mechanisms, which would indeed require a more thorough desire for transformation.

Chinese netizens express that they feel crushed and disrespected by Chinese and Western models of control alike. For instance, it became apparent during the China Google incident of 2010 that the vying owners of the Internet – the dictatorial governments and Internet corporations – were both spying on netizens to build their networks of power and control. As explained by Tricia Wang:

> Google and China have their own visions for the social life of information and for the role of information in society. We should be equally critical of a corporation with algorithms that create a consensual consumer culture based on advertising clicks as we are of a country with policies that create a consensual citizenry based on obedience through a paternalistic form of governance. (Wang 2010)

Netizens should be critical of both of these seemingly-opposed power blocs as their browsing paths are continually tested and modulated by archaic government rhetoric and an expansionist consumer culture.

Rather than relying on massive corporate networks or popular culture for social change, smaller cross-border initiatives may be more useful in creating a vibrant media culture. Rebecca MacKinnon has noted that, despite the Internet being a globalizing force, online media communities have had "a natural tendency to focus inward toward the local rather than outward across borders" (MacKinnon 2009: 11). MacKinnon argues for the locally-oriented protection and improvement of civil liberties while being inspired by models of cross-border activism and solidarity. One example of this type of civil disobedience can be found in the work of Hong Kong activist Oiwan Lam. "Don't Turn Hong Kong into a Mono-coloured Ghost City" was the title of a famous Internet article posted by Lam in 2007. Lam believed that Hong Kong's sex culture was threatened by a tunnel-vision mentality fostered by its rapidly-expanding hyper materialism. In an interview with the website Interlocals.net, Lam criticized the Obscene Articles Tribunal and argued that Hong Kong is losing its identity as a multicultural city by adopting the ideals of conservative-bourgeois materialism. (Lam 2007) In an act of civil disobedience, she urged web users to post pornographic hyperlinks on the local indie media server in order to protest against Hong Kong's growing materialism and tightening obscenity laws. Lam herself uploaded an artistic photograph of a naked woman by Jake Applebaum that she had found on the social networking and photography-sharing site Flickr. This act of civil disobedience was tracked down by conservative citizens who filed a complaint to the Obscene Articles Tribunal (淫褻物品審裁處/淫審法庭) and Wan was then prosecuted for breaking obscenity laws.

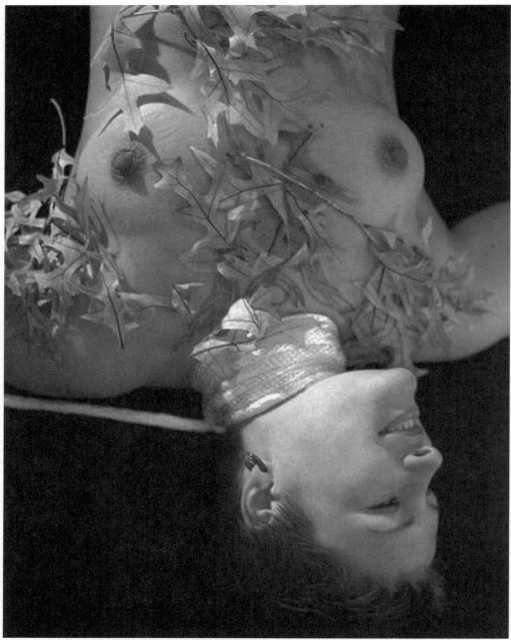

Figure 3. Photograph by Jake Applebaum, hyperlinked by Oiwan Lam to the Hong Kong Inmedia server. Lam was sued for linking to this photograph by the Hong Kong Obscene Articles Tribunal (0AT).

Lam meticulously documented her court case on her blog and other international websites in order to criticize these developments in Hong Kong sex culture. As we can understand from her conflict with local organizations, Internet activism has paved the way for a unique type of international discussion and support.

The era of user-generated Internet content also allows netizens and micro-groups to represent their sexual bodies and to distribute sexually explicit materials. Pornography has moved away from a male-oriented consumer market and has become a medium for other user groups such as women and queers to define sexual selves within media networks. There is also room for artists and activists to open up and critique the homogeneous products of transnational commerce. Web users can suggest new definitions and aesthetic variations of the body and body types, while pornography can move away from the more predictable sites and products. Besides revealing the interplay between empowerment and abjection within these cultures of mobility, this book addresses the need for locating new possibilities for Chinese eroticism. It searches for a specific erotic heritage amongst a wealth of contemporary products and lifestyles that are still dominated by overseas markets. Since these markets do not necessarily promote a knowledge of cultural differences, it is important for Chinese sex culture to embrace local histories of pornography or artistic eroticism.

For instance, art critic Bourree Lam makes a plea for the revival of the Hong Kong film industry's glory days of soft-core erotica or *Fengyue* films (風月片). This unique collection of 1970s' movies produced by the Shaw Brothers has soft-erotic tales for the general theater-goer that also incorporate other film genres. These movies can be seen as an artistically-developed and pornographic imagination. (Lam 2009) Yau Ching (游靜) has shown the importance of recovering these erotic movies, as in the work of *fengyue* film maker Li Han-hsiang (李翰祥) who reworked seventeenth-century tales of licentiousness from the late Ming Dynasty (Yau 2010: 118). For example, in his movies and newspaper columns, Li was at times inspired by female outcast personalities such as the famous Shanghai courtesan Wang Wenlan, a high-class prostitute who could attract powerful males and would openly comment on their sexual performance or the size of their genitals. Some of Li's female characters differ from the model of female sexual subjugation as they are "endowed with sharp-sightedness, courage to both love and hate, a strong sense of self-determination, and a feisty can-do-it-all spirit; they are shrews, sluts, dreamers and fighters at once" (Yau 2010: 120). These go-getting characters offer positive alternatives to the overly-clichéd and generic tropes of gender and sexual allure in male-oriented erotic cinema and commercial pornography. They show signs of a spiritualized sexuality that expands and deconstructs flattened visions of gender and sexual compatibility. They also contest overly-moralistic points of view and the practices of procreative heterosexuality. The styles and themes of these movies are refreshing and make room for honest depictions of Chinese "colorful" fantasies.

This book also seeks to discuss new waves of DIY pornography and associated mass media scandals, which allow people to both snoop on sexual novelties and contemplate sexual excesses. Attitudes of curiosity and condemnation accompany these mediated sex scandals, allowing people to get educated about media and sexuality. Mainland China attempts to stigmatize sex and pornography by equating it with excessive Internet use. The questionable psychological diagnosis of "online addiction" is rampant and Internet culture as such is equated with a severe threat to Confucianism – its uniquely Chinese character and idealized sense of responsible personhood. In "Just Like the Qing Empire: Internet addiction, MMOGs, and moral crisis in Contemporary China," Golub and Lingley (2008) show that online anti-addiction campaigns reveal a social unease concerning foreign cultural infiltration and its poisonous influences (如鸦片般滲入\毒害中國的外來文化. China's cosmopolitanism has engendered parallel visions of decay and downfall. Online addiction (上网成瘾) and Internet culture itself are located as a source of evil. The youth mobs who excel in these lifestyles and frames of mind are described with the verb "pao" (泡) – a state of mind experiencing decay and exhaustion like the bubbling but quickly-fading effervescence of a soft drink. Golub and Lingley describe this diagnosis this way:

> To a certain extent, we can say that Internet addicts "fritter" away their time at Internet cafes, but pao can also be translated as "to steep" (the action performed by tea leaves in boiling water) as an image of dissolution of concentrated efficacy and flavor out of the body into the wider environment. (Golub 2008: 70)

In recent years scholars have become more adept at deconstructing a rhetoric of pathology associated with online addiction. Several leading academic publishers have now issued ethnographic studies about what it means to be immersed in virtual communities such as *Second Life* (第二人生) and *World of Warcraft* (魔兽世界). Within this area of virtual world immersion, sociologists and anthropologist are interested in rethinking the spaces between online fantasy and physical spaces. (Anderson 2010) Bonnie Nardi has investigated collaborations amongst World of Warcraft gamers in the USA and China, as they occupy a digital-physical ecology influenced by socio-economics, government regulations and cultural value systems. Nardi has also dissected her own life and experiences as Night Elf Priest in World of Warcraft in order to get a deeper and embodied understanding of the peculiarities of human play and its social behaviors (Nardi 2010: 6).

In a similar manner, the different chapters of this book will present various incarnations of people's sexual immersion and how it has empowered, and conflicted with, their identities. Chapter 1, "The Cyber Yellow Disaster: From the Everyday Gaze to Nation-State Espionage," introduces the changes in sex industries and commercial porn sites that affect consumption in mainland China. This chapter posits that China is living in a joyful era of "people's pornography" and media activism despite government warnings about a "cyber yellow disaster" (網絡黃禍). At the same time, the ubiquitous gaze of government-imposed censorship and its attendant sex-negative rhetoric has been internalized and atomized by multiple instances of netizen-driven surveillance and sex-phobic governance. The chapter also presents the work of artists and netizens who uncover China's burgeoning sex/porn industries. For instance, the undercover researcher Tiantian Zheng created a double identity to explore and comment on previously-hidden territories of sex work. Her work shows that sex work in karaoke bars is developed in collaboration with government officials, despite their official rhetoric of extinction of these sex industries. A second site of contestation is the creative adaptation of the already-noted mythical animal, Grass Mud Horse that was named in order to protest against the government decision to have all home PC computers installed with a "youth escort filtering" system. A third example is presented in the work of artists Siu Ding (小丁) and Yu Na (俞娜), who challenge the gaze of patriarchy and average morality through unusual representations of seduction and nudity.

Chapter 2, "The Pride and Pettiness of Sex Bloggers," investigates what types of blogging discourses and what kind of sexual-liberation fantasies are being activated or dismissed in China. Citizen journalists and confessional diarists alike address the discrepancy between sexual energy and the "propaganda of impotence" (Han Han). The chapter discusses the work of leading activists Zhai Minglei (翟明磊), Tiger temple (老虎廟 lao hu miao), Han Han (韓寒) and Ai Wei Wei (艾未未). Even though this tradition of blogging is primarily focused on civil liberties, most bloggers also cover topics of pornography and sex work. In addition to a quest for freedom of expression, there has also been a growing cult of writers and artists who openly depict their unconventional private sex lives and sexual desires. Sex bloggers such as Mu Zi Mei (木子美), Hairong Tian Tian (海容天天) and Hooligan Swallow (流氓燕) radicalize the blogging mission through witty self-photography and sex diaries. Meanwhile, as also indicated in Chapter 1, a sensibility of intolerance and moral arrogance shapes itself around their digital provocations. Netizens squads or vigilantes (sometimes entitled Human Flesh Search Engine (人肉搜索) search for private, potentially-embarrassing information about celebrities and political authorities in order to pass moral judgment on them. While bloggers are fighting for a new individualism and defense of eccentricity, theirs acts are still easily condemned by a peculiar kind of mob mentality.

Chapter 3, "Gender Variations on the Aching Sex Scene," analyzes the potential of pornography as a politically transgressive force and educational tool by soliciting views and experiences of young adults from mainland China and Hong Kong. Through in-depth interviews with 60 university students, aged 18–25, and an anonymous fixed-response survey carried out on the Internet between July 2007 and May 2009, an analysis is made of male and female self-articulations of sexual pleasure and civil rights.

Now that female and males have entered, and responded to, the era of DIY pornography, what attitudes and subjectivities do they wish to maintain around the porn culture? Several schools of clinical psychologists have located gender differences in how males and females might be aroused by sexually explicit images. While women are thought to be more flexible and bi-curious in their arousal patterns, both straight and homosexual men are more likely to desire stable niche industries and images. While these findings are interesting and stimulating, little effort was made to factor in questions about sexual freedom and moral tolerance within specific cultures. Since Chinese women have been largely unable to access and enjoy pornographic products, their attitudes of consumption are, on the whole, more tentative and cautious. Women's specific cultural histories of viewing erotica are important in understanding their desire for a different type of pornography. The chapter shows that Chinese women resist the commonly-accepted Chinese tastes and products by participating in global flows of debate and diversified notions of art and pornography.

Chapter 4, "Lizzy Kinsey and the Adult Friendfinders: An Ethnographic Case-Study about Pornographic Self-Representation and Internet Sex," is based on an extensive case study in which I functioned as a participant, observer, and interviewer of selected members of the massive sex- and dating website http://www.adultfriendfinder.com. The aim was not only to analyze the changing Chinese sex climate but also to get actively involved as lustful participant within this Internet sex environment. By taking on a sexualized personality, women and men from diverse cultural backgrounds shared their unusual sexual experiences and escapades by means of online communication and face-to-face interviews. The chapter critically assesses the site's emancipator rhetoric by unraveling these testimonies and by analyzing its user-generated web content.

Chapter 5, "It Runs in the Rotten Family: Queer Love Amongst Animation Fans and Costume Players, " delves into Chinese fandom of Japanese animation and how fan groups are constructing their own sexualized identities. The creators of virtual fantasy worlds exhibit flamboyant appearances that endorse queerness as "eccentricity" and "abjection" within their social networks. They wish to escape from restrictive regional morality, but also try to fulfill the demands of high consumerism or the patriarchal corporate guidelines of the nation state. Hence, the chapter shows that they are caught up in a fuzzy quest for alternate realities and queer selves that can only be denied when facing the demands of the family, or the professional duties of actual life. The sexual fantasies and personas developed by these fan mobs are an important force in a Chinese quest for sexual pleasure and "people's pornography." They often cause the most stringent patriarchal backlash as governments ridicule or censor their unabashed devotion to Japanese culture and soft-core sex entertainment. But their fantasized love stories are part of a will to gain knowledge and a unique type of sexual entertainment.

References

Anderson, Nate (2010) "Sociologists invade World of Warcraft," 11 May, http://arstechnica.com/tech-policy/news/2010/05/sociologists-invade-world-of-warcraft-and-see-humanitys-future.ars (accessed 11 July 2011).

Feng, Chien-san (2009) "Between Alternative and Mainstream, Independence and Nationhood," in Lam Oi-Wan and Ip Iam-Chong (eds) *Info Rhizome: report on independent media in the Chinese-speaking world*, Hong Kong: In-Media.

Holmes, Brian (2008) "One World, One Dream: China at the Risk of New Subjectivities," 8 January, http://brianholmes.wordpress.com/2008/01/08/one-world-one-dream/ (accessed 11 July 2011).

Hu, Yong (2009) "Why Remain Independent and How to Be Alternative?" in Lam Oiwan and Ip Iam-Chong (eds.) *Info Rhizome: report on independent media in the Chinese-speaking world*, Hong Kong: In-Media.

Golub, Alex and Lingley, Kate (2008) "Just Like the Qing Empire: Internet addiction, MMOGs, and moral crisis in Contemporary China," in *Games and Culture*, 3: 1, pp. 59–75.

MacKinnon, Rebeca (2009) "Independent Media in the Chinese-speaking world," in Lam Oiwan and Ip Iam-Chong (eds) *Info Rhizome: report on independent media in the Chinese-speaking world*, Hong Kong: In-Media.

Lam, Bourree (2009) "Money Shots: A Look at the Hong Kong Porn Industry," *Time Out Hong Kong* (online), 13 October, http://www.timeout.com.hk/feature-stories/features/28969/money-shots-a-look-at-the-hong-kong-porn-industry.html (accessed 11 July 2011).

Lam, Oiwan (2007) "Don't Turn Hong Kong into a Mono-Colour Ghost City," Interview with Oiwan Lam, *Interlocals* (online), 2 July. http://interlocals.net/?q=node/118 (accessed 11 July 2011).

Li, Yinhe, (2010) Video interview about Swinging Professor Ma, *Joy.cn*, 21 May, http://news.joy.cn/2010/njjzyl/ (accessed 11 July 2011).

Nardi, Bonnie (2010) *My Life as Night Elf Priest*, Ann Arbor: University of Michigan Press.

Pasquinelli, Matteo (2009) *Animal Spirits: A Bestiary of the Commons*. Rotterdam: Nai and Institute of Network Cultures.

Rofel, Lisa (2007) *Desiring China: Experiments in Neoliberalism, Sexuality, and Public Culture*. Durham: Duke University Press.

South China Morning Post (SCMP) (2010) "1,332 Guilty of Spreading Porn," 6 November.

Sheller, Mimi (2007) "Virtual Islands: Mobilities, Connectivity, and the New Caribbean Spatialities," *Small Axe* 24, October, pp. 16–33.

Wang, Tricia (2010) "Googlist Realism: the Google-China Saga Posits Free-Information Regimes as a New Site of Cultural imperialism and Moral Tensions," *CulturalBytes.com*, July 10, http://culturalbytes.com/post/7818762.73/googoochinasaga (accessed 11 July 2011).

Williams, Sue (1997) *China: A Century of Revolution*. Zeitgeist Films, Information available at http://www.zeitgeistfilms.com/film.php?directoryname=chinaacenturyofrevolution (accessed 11 July 2011).

Wong, Edward (2010) "18 Orgies Later, Chinese Swinger Gets Prison Bed." *New York Times* (online), 20 May, http://www.nytimes.com/2010/05/21/world/asia/21china.html (accessed 17 July 2010).

Yau, Ching (2010) "Porn Power: Sexual and Gender Politics in Li Han-hsiang's *Fengyue* Films," in Yau Ching (ed) *As Normal as Possible: Negotiating Sexuality and Gender in Mainland China and Hong Kong*, Hong Kong University Press.

Chapter 1

The Cyber Yellow Disaster: From the Everyday Gaze to Nation-State Espionage

Introduction: Every Breath You Take, Every Move You Make

China is currently experiencing a joyful era of "people's pornography" (人民的色情) despite government warnings that have labeled it a "cyber yellow disaster" (網絡黃禍). The term "yellow movie" (黃色電影) in Chinese culture originally referred to films of a pornographic nature, and "cyber yellow" (網絡黃色) is the term used to refer to Internet pornography. Internet pornography will be defined here as a wide range of commercial and non-commercial online industries of eroticism and sexual labor. Chinese people participate in network culture as consumers and producers of sexually explicit media. They also contribute as critical netizens through alternative representations of the sexual body and while engaging in a quest for the expansion of civil liberties. Since ancient obscenity laws and ethical norms maintain a ban on sexually explicit media, a discrepancy emerges between the climate of excess and the authoritarian methods of intimidation and censorship.

In June 2010 the government of the Chinese Communist Party (中國共產黨政府) issued a White Paper on Internet Policy (網絡白皮書). The paper states that, in 2009, about 230 million people in China gathered information using search engines, and 240 million communicated through real-time devices. There were over 1 million bulletin board systems (bbs) and 220 million bloggers, while over 66 per cent of Chinese netizens frequently used the Internet in order to discuss various topics, express their opinions and represent their interests. As a result of this engagement, 60 per cent of netizens have a positive opinion of the fact that the government considers the Internet a manifestation of China's socialist democracy and progress.

Whereas netizens' activities are generally seen as a sign of Internet maturity and progress, the White Paper argues that the Internet has also caused an influx of harmful content. It is stated that online pornography is damaging the physical and psychological health of young people, and this is identified as a prominent public concern. The Law of the People's Republic of China on the Protection of Minors stipulates that the state shall

take measures to prevent minors from overindulging in the Internet, prohibit any organization or individual from producing, selling, renting or providing by other means electronic publications and Internet information containing pornography, violence, murder, terror, gambling or other contents harmful to minors. (Xinhua Agency 2010)

It is not made clear how or why online pornography is inherently harmful to minors, but that the thriving Chinese netizen culture ought to stay clear of the "cyber yellow danger."

Meanwhile, as government officials continue to make innovations in their tactics of control and intimidation, web users have internalized surveillance culture as an everyday social gaze and a form of moralistic commentary. In order to capture this synchronization of positive excitement and condemnation, David Lyon has proposed a theory of surveillance culture that takes into account the dispersal of nation-state power and capitalism into micro-sites of work and play. In his vision, people are practicing a gaze onto others as a way of enjoying everyday technologies, work activities and life-styles. People may be stalking upon or leering at somebody's private sex affairs and political mishaps, or they may simply be practicing care and control as "focused, systematic, and routine attention to personal details for purposes of influence, management, protection, or direction" (Lyon 2007: 14). In either case, netizens have become accustomed to using digital devices in an endless search for, and in order to gaze at, juicy news items and sexual novelties within peer groups.

Mainstream social networks such as Facebook or its Chinese equivalent Renren (人人網, renren wang; literally "everyone's network") tacitly encourage members to pry into each other's private lives as a collective routine that manifests social interest. While Facebook enjoys an unforeseen popularity in Hong Kong, it was banned in mainland China in July 2009 after a period of riots in Xinjiang province and the concomitant correspondences of Xinjiang independence activists (疆獨分子). Mainland China now primarily uses Renren, which was formerly known as the Xiaonei Network (校內網, xiaonei wang; literally "on-campus network") and currently has a membership of 22 million active users. Renren requires web users to register with their actual names and contact information, and its censorship rules are very strict, especially when it comes to tracking sensitive political keywords in its user-generated content.

Following the Chinese law against sexually explicit images, Renren administrators will routinely remove all sexually explicit images that are occasionally uploaded and shared amongst friends. This ban on sexually explicit materials in social networks is also seen in other countries, but Chinese citizens have developed a certain ease or poise about the routines of uploading and deletion. Moreover, as the White Paper on Internet Policy indicates, social commentary is officially cherished and protected as a positive value and a basic freedom. Hence, people do feel encouraged to comment on their Internet experiences, including those with sexually explicit media and censorship. For instance, a gallery of DIY sex photos was uploaded on Renren on 5 December 2009 showing a naked girl playing with stuffed animals along with other toys. Renren members responded quickly by praising the photos: "Wow … how Brave!" … "This is Crazy" … "My classmates and myself like these pictures, can you send some more" … "Wow, but when will they be deleted again?" … "Are they still here? We are witnessing an important moment in History" … "Yes indeed, hope we can keep these as great memories!"

Figure 1: Do-It-Yourself image distributed on the social network Renren, spurring comments in favor of sexual expressivity and against censorship. Digital drawing by Bonni Rambatan.

As will be shown throughout this book, sexual expressivity abounds and is taken up with ease, while sexually explicit videos and photographs are distributed and commented upon in the face of overly-reactionary governmental policies. These and other behaviors are a way of personally and collectively processing the politics of sex and artistic creativity. Artist and activist Ai Wei Wei, who was detained in April 2011, explained the aesthetics of social transformation this way: "It's about how to turn our basic right to information into a form that can be understood and expressed … These rights are related to art and creativity" (Yu 2010).

These basic forms include the sharing of sex images but also a playful rearranging of the banned terminology of sexuality (敏感詞). One way in which web users protect vulgar language expressions is by continually adapting particular words, names and expressions. Many words that are commonly used to refer to sexuality, including "Naked, Adult, Censorship, Lust, Mistress, and Sperm," are on a list of sensitive keywords and are automatically banned by major search engines (Demick 2010). Sometimes certain names are automatically deleted as well, such as the name of actress Tang Wei (湯唯) who made a notable, naked appearance in the sex scenes of Ang Lee's *Lust, Caution* (色│戒) (2008), a movie which was banned in mainland China. In response to Tang Wei's blacklisting, people allocated new names for her so that they could keep circulating the infamous sex scenes and other information about the actress. Netizens made huge efforts to circulate the banned sex scenes on their blogs, p2p forums and bbs. In some cases they made entire DIY television programs devoted to those deleted scenes. In one of these programs it was explained that mainland China had become so obsessed with the sex scenes that people were trying to mimic the sexual moves between Tang Wei and Tony Leung (梁朝偉).

The movie thus became a significant force and discourse for the erotic imagination and attracted a large fan base in China, Taiwan and Hong Kong. In my personal interviews with students and netizens, they reported that they had been deeply touched by the sex scenes. Besides the fact that these scenes became novelty items on the Internet, netizens argued that they were of much better quality than commercial pornography. Those very scenes were artistically accomplished and revealed the deep feelings of a female protagonist who is torn between her love for China and her strong feelings for a person who collaborates with the Japanese invader. Netizens and bloggers debated whether or not these scenes were gratuitous or integral to the movie. As explained by Sussany Tang, an exchange student from Shanghai:

> The sex scenes in this movie build towards a point. There are three scenes and each one adds to our understanding of sexual depth so we get a better understanding of a very complex relationship. [1]

The theme of political collaboration and fatal love appealed to general movie goers, while those eager to be exposed sexual novelties took the occasions to defend their right to voyeurism.

"People's Pornography": Chinese DIY (Do-It-Yourself) Versus Japanese AV (Adult Video)

Both women and men in China are using, and commenting on, sexually explicit media to explore novel tastes, desires, and identities, in order to grapple with edgy and sexually explicit content, and to question the socially-engrained roles of Chinese morality in the Internet age. Uploading and distributing sex videos is a risky business in China but, nevertheless, people are eager to do it. It is as if the ability to partake in discussion or to be a voyeur is one way of processing everyday moral pressures and social responsibilities. For instance, the Chinese Internet is swamped with a new line of DIY sex videos shot by young adults in everyday locations such as classrooms, bath houses, computer labs and city parks. These videos have been archived and labeled as Doors or Gates (门 men … after the USA Watergate scandal) and carry the name of the location where the scene was shot – e.g. East Building Kappa Female (東樓女), Metro Gate(地鐵門), Shanghai Wash Gate(上海洗手門), or Hunan Elevator Gate (湖南電梯門).

These online collections create the impression that all these dispersed locations are used by people to have sex secretly. In some cases, the onscreen lovers seem to be unaware of the camera, as if their carnal desire was captured by a security camera and/or uploaded by a third party. In other cases, the camera is so close to the scene of action that the couple must be aware of its presence, but they decide to project a specific ignorance of the camera while pursuing sexual bliss.

The video "East Building Kappa Female" follows a group of school boys undressing a girl in a classroom. While the video at first portrays a scene of callous bullying, the boys then start caressing and kissing the girl at great length. She gets aroused and is then seen laughing and frolicking with them. One of the boys further manipulates this rare moment by using his hand-held camera and teasing the Kappa female to respond to it. As a matter of fact, the young woman is very good at imitating a Japanese porn star who whimpers in pain and joy while being bullied into sexual action. The popularity of these DIY videos is explained as follows by Jun:

> These videos are now a novelty and are slightly in competition with the Japanese pornography. Of course it is important to make our own videos even if they look quite bad. Since everything is officially banned, then these videos fill the gap.

The DIY productions can be circulated despite government warnings and make for a perky novelty for the Chinese netizens. But it is clear that the trend is sensitive and potentially explosive when I attempt to solicit reactions. My interviewees are aware of the cyber yellow culture, but overall they would rather not discuss it. Some of my interviewees make a clear distinction between sexual freedom (性自由) and political freedom (政治自由) and believe that the former is futile and harmless, and hence more tolerated by the state. It is generally believed that the war on pornography is a flawed or doomed governmental incentive against the general public or a shield used by officials to step up its general surveillance technologies.

Still, despite the difficulties in conducting my interviews around pornography, people agree that it can be a powerful and important incentive for social change. Yang explained it this way:

> We have a common saying that if virtue rises one foot, vice will rise ten. The government will always have its policies against sex but we always know how to find it.

Yang is attached to his ways of "Jumping the Great Fire Wall" (翻牆) and searching for sexually explicit materials on illegal peer-to-peer downloading sites such as Emule and Bittorrent. Rather than hoping that central government will legalize and organize his online pleasures through e-commerce, he is devoted to the supplies within these shadow industries. He adds that he even gets educational benefits from these movies, as he learns, for instance, how to kiss and caress girls. He explains that it is very hard to get any information about sex acts in China and that pornography is the one way men can try and learn about how to become better lovers.

Within the larger struggles for civil liberties and sex education going on throughout China, netizens protect the sexual body as a private refuge of pleasure and awareness. Pornographic materials are quite routinely tracked and deleted by web administrators, but they are re-uploaded on migratory websites. Even though these sites are flourishing hubs of culture and commerce with huge impact on Internet culture, they are officially non-existent and/or volatile due to possible and immediate erasure. In April 2010 alongside the opening of the Shanghai World Expo, the Bureau of Press and Publication (新聞出版總署) issued a statement that "A Hard Fist Will Clamp Down on the Cyber Yellow Disaster." The title of one of the posts stated that: "The Anti-pornography and Anti-illegal Publications Office will launch a Green Bookmark Project". This was yet another massive effort to ban all pirated materials and all pornographic products. The action supposedly led to a confiscation of more than 65,958 million illegal publications in the year 2009, 1,443 million of which were pornographic in nature, while 56,844 million were pirated products in general (Xie 2010).

But despite these large-scale actions, there is still a steady growth in the pornography industries. Scholars at the Department of Computer Science and Technology at Xi'an Jiaotong University have confirmed that the Chinese Internet is swamped with sites for pornography (Wu 2010). They used two different online monitoring systems, an advanced web crawler and pornographic content monitor, to search the mainland China Internet between 29 March 2009 and 25 January 2010. They found that there is a steady rise in the number of websites even though a large percentage of this gradual expansion is regularly swept up by the government. They registered about two thousand sites in one segment of a Western Province, while speculating that much larger numbers are located around the Eastern coastal regions and the more developed cities of Beijing, Shanghai and Guanzhou. It was also found that 93.2 per cent of pornography sites are run from web servers that are located abroad. Finally, they found that only a small percentage of regular pornography

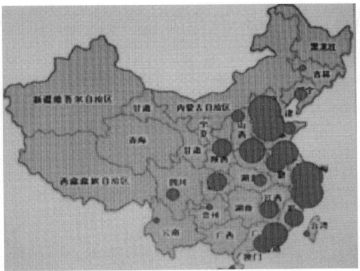

Figure 2: Geographic Distribution of Pornography sites in China.

users prefer hardcore materials, while a large majority of users infrequently look for a wider variety of materials.

In "Sexual Behavior in China: Trends and Comparisons" it was equally confirmed that mainland China has seen a boom in pornography and sexual entertainment (Parish et al. 2007). A large-scale survey was carried out by the China Health and Family Life Survey (中國家庭健康狀況調查) that collected data from about five thousand people in 60 neighborhoods in China's adult population aged 20–64 years (with the exclusion of Tibet and Hong Kong). Researchers used a combination of computer-assisted, self-administered statements and face-to-face interviews to get responses from, and also concerning, different age groups or generational "cohorts." It was found that the post-1980s' and post-1990s' generations (八十後和九十後) have indeed gone through a spectacular increase in the use of private sex, sexual entertainment and pornography. For instance, younger males specifically report a much younger age at which they first masturbate, have sexual intercourse or use commercial sex services. This is different from non-Chinese cultures such as the USA or France, where commercial sex services such as peep shows and sex workers are more commonly used by older generations. As for Chinese attitudes towards sexually explicit media, it was found that 75 per cent of men and 25 per cent of women within the younger generation are remarkably more at ease with matters of pornography. Based on these changes, the report concluded that "a sexual revolution" is occurring in China as the 1980s' and 1990s' generations have a drastically-different outlook on matters of sexuality than the older generation.

China's leading sexologist Pan Siuming (潘綏銘) has argued that the sexual revolution is not primarily triggered by economic reforms and the influx of overseas materials. His own comprehensive survey about sexual relations and behaviors in 2000 points to radical changes in the primary life cycle that started before the era of economic form. The primary life cycle does not posit sex as an autonomous category but refers to a totality of functions and relations between the most fundamental aspects of human activity such as gender, love, maturation and child-rearing. The primary life cycle went through its most radical change after the Cultural Revolution when the concept of romantic love was liberated from associations with petit-bourgeoisie sentiment. Concepts of love and sexual pleasure were further revitalized with the introduction of the one-child family (1981), which completely challenged the traditional equation of sex with procreation. One of the consequences of the new life cycle is a more energetic sex-life, including practices of recreational sex, extra-marital sex and a deeper attachment to pornography (Siuming 2006).

The female and male interviewees interviewed for this book have experienced several decades of economic reform and sexual revolution. They are the young adults of the hyper-wired generation but they are mostly quite shy and hesitant to discuss pornography. Nonetheless, they are familiar with the products and also quite cynical or dismissive of bombastic clean-up campaigns and their underlying methods of surveillance. Many of them feel free enough to cooperate with me, testifying that the porn culture is alive and well on the streets and on the Internet. As Jello explains:

In China, they are called "movies about life (生活電影). They are actually movies about sex and you can find vendors in most cities. They will typically lead you to a small corner where not so many people pass and they will pull out all their discs.

To the present day in China, the bulk of adult entertainment consists of pirated Japanese adult videos (盜版日本成人電影) distributed through bootleg VCD production and Internet sites. The local markets of Japanese AV in China, Hong Kong and Taiwan have flourished as bootleggers have responded to localized taste by mixing together selections (Yau and Wong 2009). Moreover, the imported Japanese videos are mostly hardcore pornography that does not contain digitized mosaics placed over the genitals. They are taken from Japanese underground and bankruptcy markets that have bypassed the obscenity standards set by the Japanese NEVA (Nihon Ethics of Video Association), which would prescribe that genital areas and pubic hair are blurred by means of such mosaics. These "movies about life" have been sold and distributed illegally for decades, making a significant impact on Chinese youngsters, their sexual knowledge and desires.

To further test the accessibility and livelihood of Internet pornography, despite the governmental rhetoric of extinction, a surfing experiment was conducted in one of the Starbucks coffee shops in Shenzhen, which is one of China's border towns directly across the border from Hong Kong. Most of these coffee shops now offer a free wifi connection and do not have a firewall beyond the one imposed by the central government. I traveled from

Hong Kong to Shenzhen with a team of collaborators willing to test the efficiency of the new anti-pornography campaigns. Once installed with the Starbucks concoction called "green tea frappucino," it took us approximately five to ten minutes to find a wide range of hardcore and DIY images by means of the search engine Baidu.

We typed in the keyword 開心色情網 (Happy Pornography Website), or KXSQW, which led to a forum where customers posted new URLS for one of the largest migrating websites. One of those sites pretends to be a legal Hong Kong site, but the characters and language reveals that is an illegal mainland site. It branches off into different commercial listings like "Butterfly Vagina" (蝴蝶陰道)" or "Young Face" (年輕容顏) and DIY pornography listings such as "School Girl Private Photography" (學生妹私照), "Middle School Taiwanese with Angel Face" (天使面孔台灣高中生,), "Sex on the Persian Carpet." (波斯地毯上的性事)

Of course it would be unlikely for regular costumers to be accessing pornography in a coffee shop such as Starbucks, but the ease with which we could track down images and videos pointed to the existence of illegal porn industries. It was quite easy to get access to sexually explicit materials and most of the products we could find were indeed a mixture of commercial Japanese videos and Chinese DIY products.

We also tracked down a copy of *Country Uncle and Country Girl* (農民伯伯鄉下妹), one of China's first amateur features making waves on the Internet. The story of the movie reflects the climate of social unrest and taboo discussed in this chapter. It is typically Chinese story of a "country uncle" (or a farmer) and a strange character, Uncle Chow, who visits the farmer's home and claims that he owes him a lot of money. Uncle Chow also manages to seduce the farmer's daughter, and then her parents agree that she should just marry him to clear their debt. Uncle Chow is the bastard child of a village woman who was raped by a man and was drowned by the villagers for that reason. As an orphan child, he became a mysterious and unhinged character. Towards the end of the movie, uncle Chow reveals his life-story and declares that it is time for him to take revenge. He pulls out a gun and insists that the father make love with his daughter in front of him and the mother. The farmer obeys and uncle Chow watches for a while and then rapes the mother of his newly-wed wife.

This movie is aesthetically- and philosophically-crude and shows the eroticization of primitive and patriarchal countryside morality. The fantasy story deals with rural incest taboos and reflects pre-modern life-styles that have gone through a turbo overhaul into modernization.

The online movie reviews are mixed, as some customers clearly prefer Japanese professionalism over Chinese DIY:

It's an interesting story, but it is pretty fake. The actresses are not professional and they cannot be compared to Japanese actresses. The shooting is also pretty slow and the director's directions even appear in the movie. If you listen to it carefully, you can hear the director saying 'kiss here, touch there!' you can actually hear that!

UNIVERSITY OF WINCHESTER LIBRARY

Figure 3: Browsing Experiment in Shenzhen Starbucks, Spring 2010. Sexually explicit websites and images were within easy access despite the total ban on pornography.

Figure 4: Stills from one of China's first amateur feature-length pornography movie, *Country Uncle and Country Girl*. Date and name of directors and actors are unknown.

Another person disagrees and defends the Chinese flavor of the story:

> As a first Chinese AV, it's great that it has such complex plot and it also proves that the Chinese people have emotional issues and unique pressures. Even if it is AV, it has so many Chinese features in it and it is so different from the European, American or Japanese ones.[2]

Even if one can get easy access to pornographic products on the Chinese Internet, the new wave of Chinese DIY pornography is still quite thin and the pornographic landscape is mostly dominated by Japanese AV. A series of interviews I made with male pornography consumers in Hong Kong shows that Chinese men are mostly hooked on Japanese pornography and porn stars rather than either Chinese or Western stars. In probing the reasons why they want Japanese pornography, one could point to obvious reasons of easy access to overseas markets and the stigmatization of local sex workers. Since there is a shortage of local productions and pornography stars within the Chinese cultures, the sexual imagination has been hijacked by a peculiar kind of erotic-cultural imperialism. A reclaiming of Chinese sexual bodies through home-made pornography content (家庭自製情色) would be important to even up a dominant scripting of eroticism and perversity by overseas producers. The most common reasons cited by men adoring Japanese pornography stars is their familiarity with "yellow" skinned actresses – Asian faces, tiny body figures, "proper" femininity and a dislike of sexually-aggressive or "coarse" women in Western pornography. These qualities of the female simply allow Chinese men to feel sexually competent and appreciated. Male interviewees did admit that they like to project a patriarchal viewpoint onto female models, whereby strategies of dominance or violence are used to arouse women. One of the localized AV actresses in the late 1990s was Yuki Maiko (夕樹舞子), who embodied the cute bishojo girl ideal (美少女), in titles such as *Loss of Virginity* (1996) or *The Sexual School Life: Yuki Maiko* (Wong 2009: 11–14).

One of the most popular Japanese stars on the Internet today is Sola Aoi (蒼井空), a stereotype of youthful beauty but with the addition of cyber-cultural finesse. She became known for "having brought down China's Great Firewall" when she turned into a fervent micro-blogger on Twitter in 2010 and managed to motivate thousands of Chinese fans to access her banned website (Ottomo 2010). Aoi responds to her Chinese fan base by uploading photographs and tweeting daily, by learning the Chinese language and by participating in fan meet-ups that take place in China.

A second reason for the Chinese preference for Japanese pornography is based on deep-seated political tensions between China and Japan. Lu Wang, an undergraduate student from Beijing, tells me that he likes to watch the subjugation of Japanese women because it expresses his latent desire for revenge over the Japanese and their history of dominance over China. To make his point clear he has brought along a Chinese graffiti tag that says "Fuck Jap! (操日本)," showing a Chinese animation character Cucurbit Boy, a household name for the post-80s' generation, having sex with the Japanese animation character Astro

Figure 5: Japanese AV actress Yuki Maiko who conformed to the "pure girl" archetype and had a huge fanbase in 1990s' Hong Kong and China. Digital drawing by Bonni Rambatan.

Figure 6: Japanese AV actress Sola Aoi who has a
large online fanbase in China in 2010-2011 and is
known to have "brought down the great firewall."
Digital drawing by Bonni Rambatan.

Figure 7: Popular graffiti tag expresses a Chinese revenge fantasy as the Chinese cartoon character Cucurbit Boy takes The Japanese icon Atom Boy from behind.

Boy (鐵臂阿童木). Chinese men perhaps like to be paired with a lover or sex object who embodies decency and helplessness. The Japanese porn star also often fits this ideal as she acts out decorous beauty through archetypes of the bishojo girl (美少女), or a cute and courtly young girl, who is often dressed as a submissive waitress, Lolita (洛麗塔) or schoolgirl (學生妹). Hence, it seems that both the Chinese DIY and the Japanese AV movies are adept at maintaining a traditional view of gender and power. Even if sexually explicit media are used and shared by netizens to defend civil liberties, the products themselves mostly reveal patriarchal fantasies, taboos, and frustrations.

Sexual Liberation and the Patriarchal Grip

China's premier sex researcher Dr. Li Yinhe Professor at the Chinese Academy of Social Sciences (中国社科院教授李银河), explains that contemporary China can be characterized by a rift between its capitalist-utopian visions and its ancient obscenity laws:

There is the old Yinhuipin Fa (反淫穢法則Law of Obscenity), which is an article in the criminal law stating that producing, selling or spreading obscene matters is prohibited. So the ban on online materials is based on this law. I think that this law is outdated and it is erroneous, because it contradicts the law of freedom of speech and publications which is also part of the constitution. In China, there are a lot of laws like that. They are obviously outdated but they are still in effect. As a result there is an ongoing conflict between the people and the government. For quite a long time there have been two kinds of attitudes crashing against each other. We have the people who want to support these obscenities, and we have the government who doesn't want them to release their desires. [3]

Blogger Zhang resonates with the views of Dr. Li Yinhe and complains that the Chinese Internet has locked up his sex drive by building a "walled culture." As he explains:

The economic reform in China has 30 years of history but China is still under the cycle of the "damned wall." One of the greatest deeds in our reform is the liberation of our body. While government officials can openly patronize prostitutes, buy second wives and use government funded stipends to visit red night districts in foreign countries, netizens' most humble pleasure is getting access to pornographic websites … But our Internet monitoring system can detect our private details like a piece of cake. All online interactions, communications, love talks or dirty jokes become visible and can be traced back to the original sender. (Zhang 2010)

Despite the fact that bloggers and activists are tired of censorship and have derisively called the Chinese Internet "a net to catch people," the consumption of sexual entertainment and pornography is still on the rise. When China opened its door to the yellow culture in the early 1980s, there was a concomitant campaign against spiritual pollution (清除精神污染運動). Government warnings and actions against sexually explicit media have consistently been issued, but the PPC is simultaneously pursuing a new world dream that leans towards neo-liberalism. The nature of this dream is crudely materialistic and technotopian while still depriving people, in contrast to the West, of a more open and confident sex culture.

Web sites and social networks have enabled sex workers to set up small-scale businesses and to create more direct arrangements with clients. In this sense, sex culture includes a move towards self-representation and pleasure despite the official stringent laws against sexualized commodities. In her study of American sex industries, *Temporarily Yours; Intimacy, Authenticity, and The Commerce of Sex*, Elizabeth Bernstein explains that the boundaries between authentic intimacy and purchased sexual transactions in contemporary cultures are in flux. She postulates the existence of a recreational sexual ethic and sensibility, which is no longer antagonistic to the sphere of public commerce and involves a search for deep physical sensations and intimate erotic exchanges (Bernstein 2007: 6). This type of intimacy would be free of reproductive consequences and long-term love attachments, and more securely enclosed within the frame of one or several encounters. Some services, such as those that provide upscale escorts, have come to resemble the experiences of private love affairs, allowing clients to have deeper relationships with their temporarily-purchased lovers.

In the Chinese context, there has been a similar blurring of boundaries between a commodified and/or personally-satisfying sexual experience. For instance, some upscale escorts in Singapore manage complex lifestyles that involve intense sexual-emotional bonds. While these sex industries are officially shunned by Singapore's authorities, hostesses develop profitable businesses through complex and intimate relationships with clients. Clients use these industries to have quality physical experiences and express a kind of devotion that they often cannot express at home. In the remarkable testimonies compiled by Gerrie Lim, escorts reveal intimate details about the nature of these relationships and how they benefit financially *and* emotionally (Lim 2004).

Recreational sex has also melded into mainland Chinese life-styles as it serves a new entrepreneurism and a rite of passage or a status-enhancement practice amongst male elite groups. Zheng Tiantian's study *Red Lights: The Lives of Sex Workers in Postsocialist China* shows that sex industries are beneficial to female workers but also reinforce the patriarchal control mechanisms of the nation state (Zheng 2009: 105). The post-Mao purchase of sexual services was a reaction to the extreme asceticism in government planning of the 1950s and 1960s. Chinese Men started to revolutionize their life-styles and to reclaim their youth by being sexually active within the new sex industries. Zheng complements Pan Siuming's optimistic views about the Chinese sexual revolution by revealing larger control mechanisms and lack of autonomy amongst workers and clients. As an undercover researcher and participatory ethnographer, she worked as a hostess and befriended the sex workers and their clients. Her self-immersed report shows that men and women bond and thrive in these bars, but also become victims of police brutality and government interference.

According to her interviews, men are not looking only for extra-marital bliss or societal rebellion, but they feel pressured and coerced to act out a complex chain of social obligations; the visits to bars which prostitutes frequent are a symbolic way for men to bond with their business partners or to pay tribute to a group of alliance members. It is a matter of social etiquette which, in previous years, would have been carried out over banquets of food. Men reinforce the hierarchal manner of conducting business affairs by way of dating and mating hostesses. For instance, the selection of sex workers when entering the bar is done in such a way that the leader of a company or political group picks a hostess first, to be followed by the second- and third-ranked males, and so on. The sex workers are seen as sidekicks who may have their own magical appeal but are fundamentally not respected; they are easily cast aside and abused. Within the male-centered ritual, loyalty or love for the sex workers is seen as a weakness which clients must struggle to avoid.

Secondly, this ritual involves a symbolic regulation of male semen (精液) as vital fluids. Since the initiation of the one-child policy (計劃生育) in 1979 male semen has been subconsciously devalued by the state, but takes on a special meaning amongst female partners. Under traditional Taoist ideology, semen is the most essential element for sustaining men's life and vitality. The wives of sex clients, therefore, do not forbid adultery but they tolerate it as long as they are able to catch their fair share of vital fluids or *jing* (精). As Zheng explains:

> The chief managerial duty of the male is the allocation of assets between the wife and the hostesses he visits. The wife will try to deplete her husband of *jing*, but this is also impossible in the Taoist tradition. The hidden production of *jing* within the male body makes it impossible for wives to determine with certainty whether they have successfully drained their husbands' *jing* supply. (Zheng 2008: 120)

Through interviews with clients, Zheng shows that men are indeed concerned about their *jing* supply and believe that they can improve its quality by sleeping with several women, or specifically with young women or virgins. While Confucian morality taught them that they need to share life and sex with their wives, they also acknowledge the older Taoist sex laws and manners. They may also be disillusioned with their wives and seek strength and refuge in relationships with sex workers.

Even though there is plenty of open information about sexual entertainment in China, the Chinese government is very careful to control the debates around this topic. A good example would be SARFT's (State Administration of Radio, Film and Television [國家 廣播電影電視總局]) banning of *Woju* (蝸居), a popular TV soap opera about a wealthy man and his mistress or "second wife" (二奶), which was first aired on several local TV stations, including Dragon TV (Shanghai) and Beijing TV Youth Channel. The TV show tells the story of a Shanghai-based young woman, Haizao, who wants to help her sister buy a house for her family. She starts an affair with Song, her colleague at work who is a corrupt, high-ranking official in the city. Song starts lending her huge amounts of money, which she can only repay by dedicating her body to him. Haizao slowly begins to fall for this powerful and charming middle-aged man and becomes his second wife. At the end of the series Song gets involved in manipulating the real estate market. He tragically dies in a car accident right before his arrest for corruption and thus avoids prosecution. Haizao is meanwhile pregnant with his child but Song's wife beats her, causing a miscarriage and the loss of her uterus.

Despite the catastrophic ending for the mistress in this soap, the program unleashed a deluge of reactions of support for this life choice amongst female fans. The SARFT spokesperson said that the series had to be banned because of its negative and degenerating values: "It has a very serious negative influence on our society as the producers used sex, dirty jokes and corruption stories to attract audiences" (Chang 2009). However, the ban actually sparked its status amongst fans, who were primarily younger people. They had been watching the program on TV and video-sharing websites like Youko.com and Tudo.com. An online survey was conducted on sina.com about the program and targeted young single girls with the following question: "Which one would you choose: a young guy who loves you but has nothing or an old guy who also loves you and has everything?"[4] The statisics showed that 46.2 per cent opted for the older well-connected man, while 22.2 per cent would choose the better-looking and younger guy.

In their comments many women state that they like older men who can support them financially and who are possibly even better in the bedroom. They admire the new entrepreneurial masculinity, indicating that financial stability is a higher value than the pangs of desire or the laws of romance. They desire to be partnered up with a "Big Bucks" (大款), a person who has an upper-middle lifestyle which allows him to develop a giving personality. He may not necessarily be handsome but he may be well educated and is able to make room for elaborate, affectionate sex dates. Women are on the lookout for this kind of "strategic" or "successful" romance even though they have to take the position of a submissive sexual object. As noted in the following comments:

What is love? Love is a gimmick made by man. Screw the shit like "I give my heart to you" or "I am yours forever". These are the words from penniless men, since they can afford nothing but sweet talk, which is totally worthless. If you are a real man and you love a woman, say nothing, just show her wads of bills because this secures her; and then give her a house, because that way after you fucked her she has some place to lay down her body.

Other women disagree and leave angry comments about the subjugation of women:

How to be a second wife? Do whatever you can to make yourself look naive and innocent. The rich and powerful guys are tired of watching buxom women, and now they need village dishes. It really doesn't matter if your boobs are tiny and butt flabby or you don't have a brain. Actually sometimes stupidity works.

The survey heated up the discussion about the post-eighties' and post-nineties' generations and their relative materialistic values. In this specific narrative, the main asset to be accumulated through a relationship with a wealthy partner would be real estate. As some women indicate in their playful responses:

No house (Fang-zi), no sexual intercourse (Fang-shi)

I am still in the middle of WoJu, but I have already started worrying about my future. Happiness totally depends on what you are after. Watching WoJu makes me think – if you want a house before your 30s, find yourself a sugar daddy; if you want enough money for your whole life, and also your family members' lives, become a second wife. In big cities like Beijing and Shanghai, you have to have some background. If you don't, you cannot buy a good house even if you have enough money. No one cares about you. The housing price will rise and rise. Then you want to be a slave for a house, and then you start to work like a horse …

I am not surprised to see such kinds of TV productions in this country and in this age. I watched the news today and Obama said there should be more American overseas students coming to China – 100,000 per year. 100,000 Americans per year, if two thirds are male, that would be 70,000. On the average, they can get three Chinese women per person – 200,000 women then. Of course, half of those 200,000 would be women from Shanghai, because they need to buy a house.

Other women state that they appreciate the complexity of this relationship as it is depicted in the TV series. The story of *Woju* was a breakthrough in the sense that both mistress and patron embarked on a love journey that challenged their predictable roles of male success and female dependency. Therefore, Song's character and privilege seems authentic and enriching to women, and they also like the fact that he has a sympathetic personality:

The second wife in *WoJu* should be the most glamorous second wife on screen in China. Second wives in news programs are usually represented by material girls and long-term whores. However, Haizao enlightened us on that: The second wife doesn't necessarily fall for money, they could fall for anything, even things they don't know.

What is unusual in *WoJu* is its portrayal of Song as a handsome, romantic and sophisticated hero where normally a corrupted official like him would be described very negatively. Therefore, it's not surprising to see that many women choose him on the Internet survey.

The *Woju* debate shows that Chinese youngsters are well aware of the patriarchal premises underlying the neo-liberal new world dream. It was to be expected that *Woju* would eventually cast the mistress in a negative light, as when she loses her uterus. The entrepreneurial bind of the sex industries is tolerated and supported as they offer specific benefits for both males and females. Social commentaries about this inequality and feminist interventions are still rare and show that novel sexual identities are caught up in a patriarchal universe where sexual activism, entrepreneurism and creative rebellion are more likely acted out by males.

Rumble In The Jungle: Building a Uniquely Chinese Internet

The PPC government requires web users to gain government approval before opening any website or blog, and to submit contact information when accessing social networks on the Internet. Governmental monitoring and censorship of the web primarily involves locating forbidden content, arranging visits between police officers and site administrators, shutting down host servers, and modifying pages that are linked to overseas servers. With the construction of a Golden Shield (金盾工程), later called the Great Fire Wall (網絡防火長城), a data-base-driven remote surveillance system was also created that offers immediate access to national and local records on every person in China. This system ultimately aims to integrate data from its vast surveillance networks of cameras, speech and face recognition systems, smart cards and credit records. The Chinese government did not operate in a void while building this Golden Shield as it collaborated with Western high-tech corporations who desired to expand their business into China. He Qinglian believes that the potential of a Chinese free speech Internet was actually "hijacked" by these foreign corporations who aided the Chinese government in building an imposing system of surveillance and control, also nicknamed the Chinese "Innernet." (He 2008: 170)

This system is now fully operational and also actively tested and ridiculed by anti-censorship activists. Most critics of Chinese web culture agree that it has created a creative yet inflammatory citizens culture. At the same time, Chinese web culture is increasingly controlled by rows between the Chinese government and overseas corporations. In January 2010, a conflict between the Internet search giant Google and the Chinese government revealed China's increasing control over global Internet politics and its disdain of activist web culture. Google had threatened to leave China after some of its source code along with the gmail accounts of dissidents and human rights activists had been accessed by the

Chinese government. While some Chinese web users applauded Google's bold move against the Chinese state and away from Chinese markets, others were cynical about the corporate giant's support of citizen movements. These conditions highlighted a growing rift between those in favor of Chinese neo-liberalism and those who desire to maintain a more critical, open and inclusive network culture.

The defenders of an open network culture argued that China was perfecting its cultural-technological walled fortress, or building an "Innernet" rather than an Internet. Celebrity Blogger Han Han (韓寒) was one of the popular voices defending an open Internet:

All I can say is that I really regret the Google exit. The world's outstanding websites have left us one after another, and China's Internet has changed into the world's biggest local area network. If that's how it is, I think it's a pity, anyway we all should enhance our skills – either by "jumping the GWF" (跳牆) or other techniques, let's step it up. (Han Han 2010a)

Han Han argued that people should participate in global networks and voice their cynicism and social criticism beyond the boundaries of "local area networks." Blogger Lifan complained that Chinese rights are hijacked by political elites, while ordinary citizens have to use multiple strategies while continually watching their mouths. He himself has become tired of trying to avoid being targeted by the censors:

Since I went online in 1997, I set up different online accounts with different passwords in order to protect my privacy. I learned how to jump over the GFW and access Twitter so that I could know more about the world. However, the technology for getting around censorship is getting more and more sophisticated and I have to admit that I am getting old. I can't take care of my so-called "rights" anymore. (Zhang 2010)

Many web users today regret the fact that a gap has been created between the Chinese Internet and its overseas counterparts. A student at City University eloquently summarized his three arguments against a Chinese Innernet in this way:

I will become a journalist in the future, and I just think I should be able to get good information from the Internet. But if domestic as well as international news is controlled, I can't know anymore what information to select. That is my first concern. And my second concern is that we should be able to bring the China news with our own voices, and not rely on those from the New York Times and other overseas media outlets. If we restrict our Internet, and we Chinese cannot protect our voices, then the whole world will only hear those other voices. And those are again totally different from the facts. And my third concern is that we do have a lot of scandals in China, and they should be known and corrected. The Internet is a very useful tool in this for journalists and common citizens to find information about these scandals. So I say no to censorship.

The state-level policies about protecting youth from sexually explicit media became one of the key issues in the raging debate about the Chinese Internet. Several weeks into the Google crisis in January 2010, Han Han made an act of public protest against a new obscenities law that sought to intercept and delete all vulgarities from phone text messages. He pointed out that vulgarities were valuable forms of popular art and should not become target of censorship. If other forms of high art such as classical concerts would be allowed, then it was high time to deconstruct their status and make a bid for low art. He announced that he would have to become a vulgar person from now on and start sending vulgarities to his male and female friends. He invited government officials to follow his example by clearly-articulating vulgar items in newspaper and on television:

> The relevant government department should publish in the People's Daily and read aloud on the TV news a list of the [banned] obscene and pornographic words. For example, on the news, the female announcer could say that "the relevant department has initiated a stern crackdown on pornographic messages and the vulgar-ization of texting. Words to be banned include: "Vagina," then the male announcer says "penis" … that would be a truly responsible [way of handling it]. (Han Han 2010b)

Even if pornography is somewhat less sensitive than other politically-sensitive topics, it is taken up by netizens in their expressions of cynicism and outrage against the state. For instance, in early June 2009, when it was announced that the filtering software Green Dam Youth Escort (綠壩·花季護航) would have to be installed on every computer in the PRC to protect children and minors, netizens responded almost instantly and began ridiculing the government's decision. They complained about the costs and efficiency of this software and publicized methods for uninstalling it. For instance, blogger Xue Ying reported on cnreview.com that an ordinary pupil had already found a way to crack the code and that this information would be widely circulated. In June 2009 a search for "hacking green dam" (破解綠壩) on Google had 108,000 results, while on Baidu (百度網) it had 348,000 results (Xue 2009).

While web users could have access to formulas to crack the code, young adults also became vocal about the government ban on pornography. One Chinese student at City University of Hong Kong voiced her frustrations about the software:

> Another hopelessly stupid government decision … and god knows what happened between Green Dam developers and the Ministry of Industry and Information Technology (MIIT) Are they crazy? I mean to use 40million RMB to do such thing with such dubious software.

Other Chinese students were admittedly more cynical and jaded about this episode of government censorship as they had experienced these types of conditions ever since they began using the Internet.

Around the time of the Green Dam controversies, it was reported by Xinhua News Agency (新華通訊社) that "tens of thousands of people" would be recruited to report on lewd content and uncivilized behavior on the Internet. Six months later it was announced that rewards of up to 10,000 yuan ($1,465) would be offered by Chinese authorities to web users who would troll the web and report on sites that feature pornography. The strategy met with great success, as reported by Xinhua News Agency, "... within the first 24 hours, a hotline set up by the Internet Illegal Information Reporting Centre was flooded with more than 500 phone calls and 13,000 online tips" (*Times of India* 2009). Six months later, in December 2009, it was reported that more than 5,000 arrests had been carried out, which was a four-fold increase since the year 2008 (*China Digital Times* 2009). Three months later it was announced that 9,000 pornography sites had been closed down and that the Beijing Association of Online Media (北京網絡媒體協會) would also mobilize a group of mothers to spy on the Internet and track pornographic content in order to supposedly maintain a safe Internet for children and minors.

Even though these news items suggest a top-down victory over the cyber national disaster, in actuality these figures are not representative of an actual clampdown or extinction of sexually explicit media. In a sarcastic reversal of bombastic government rhetoric, blogger Laotuzaiz suggests that the power itself ought to be monitored by mothers. As he writes:

> Why don't we change the Mama Jury into a Mama for Government Officials. Let's send our mothers to the Ministry of Health, AQSIQ, the State Administration of Industry & Commerce. Let them monitor the head of department, and the bureau and office, like the way they monitor the netizens. It would definitely work. Don't worry. And Let the mothers be under the supervision of the National Federation of Women ... Every kind of being has its natural enemy. Chinese government officials are naturally fearful of ordinary women. (Wan, Global Voices Online, 2010)

Several years before the citizens squads against pornography were recruited, the Chinese government started to hire web users or "50 cents bloggers," as they came to be known (五毛黨), who were paid to post comments that would be favorable towards government policies in order to guide and direct public opinion on various Internet platforms. As explained by an informant who worked as a "50 cents blogger," bloggers would originally be paid 50 cents for each post that they wrote. However, in reality, they could earn a lot more money as the payment rates would depend on their Internet popularity or the number of hits and comments left by other web users. For instance, if a certain post would get 1,000 responses, then there could be a payment of 1,000 yuan. To illustrate this point, my informant showed a popular video on youko.com, which she thinks has been posted by a 50 cents blogger. The video is made up of a patriotic song and photographs and makes a comparison between the soldiers of the People's Liberation Army (人民解放軍) and those of US Army (美軍). While Chinese soldiers are presented in their potent, self-effacing and supernatural capacities, American soldiers are shown having fun, smiling into the camera while reading pornographic magazines. The patriotic song, in its English translation, states:

how strong you are
you are steely
you are loyal to the people and the nation
you are high-spirited
you are like a mountain
you (the soldiers) are the heroes

The video incites people to publicly praise Chinese soldiers and, indeed, the video gets a fair amount of patriotic comments from sympathetic web users.

In some cases patriotic messages are posted by government officials who disguise themselves as ordinary web users. For instance, a new book about the benefits of guidance under the Communist party made the rounds on bbs and sold out in several weeks. It turned out that this book had been recommended by Zhu Liangcai (朱良才), the Secretary of the Zhoukou City Communist Youth League, who had posted favorable comment as an ordinary web user. Zhu defended his need for masquerade as follows:

> The reason we do not use our true identity while communicating with netizens is that we allow people to feel our mutual equality, and avoid creating a feeling of opposition. At the same time the work can be smoothly accomplished without revealing what goes on behind the scenes; and this achieves very good results. (Henan People Daily, 2009)

Mao Lei, Head of the Internet Department of the Zhoukou City Communist Youth League Committee (共青團周口市市委網絡部), added that cadres often mask themselves as ordinary web users in order to smoothly influence public opinion:

> We usually participate in online discussions using the identity of ordinary netizens. When there are uncivilized acts or inappropriate discussions, we actively admonish those who write the comments … Aside from this, we put a lot of emphasis on the work of guiding the opinions of young people, expressing correct opinions about hot current events in a timely manner. (Henan People Daily, 2009)

The members of the 50 cents army are trained and recruited to help high-ranking officials establish their goals. They are selected through the Communist Party at schools and universities. New members are instructed through weekly meetings and classes about policies and they are provided lists of sensitive topics. The informant believes that about ten other students in her department were doing the same kind of work. I asked her if she considered this job to be an honor, since she and others may hope someday to become a member of the Communist Party. She replied negatively, adding that she knows that many of her friends looked down on her activity in the 50 cents army. Her posts had been attacked by web users who despised the 50 cents army (五毛黨), which she was able to take note of even though these attacks were almost immediately deleted by site administrators. She also makes clear that she quit this position after moving to Hong Kong to become a university student. She tells me repeatedly during the interview that the topic makes her sad as she knows that the Chinese Internet has become "rubbish" or "like a dump." She also makes clear that there was some tolerance within the 50 cents army towards the existence of pornography or the "yellow culture," and that it was indeed treated differently from other sensitive topics, but overall she had become very cynical about Internet freedom in general due to the ubiquitous presence of these government-trained spies.

Internet Activism and Animal Spirits

Guobin Yang (楊國彬) is one of the leading media scholars who believes that despite cycles of government intervention, the Chinese Internet is boisterous and innovative in its ways of dealing with surveillance culture. In making this claim, he draws a distinction between the concepts of negative freedom and positive freedom and shows that online examples of humor, creativity and dissent create a culture of positive freedom. As he writes:

> In the Chinese case, policies of Internet control limit negative freedom. They are obstacles to free speech. Yet under the conditions of contracting negative freedom, Chinese Internet users choose neither resignation nor apathy nor despair. Instead, the history of Internet development in the past 15 years shows that the more negative freedom is curtailed, the more engaged Chinese netizens are in the struggle for Internet expression and the more creative that expression becomes. Thus, as the Great Firewall gets more sophisticated, so do netizens' skills for scaling it. (Yang 2010)

Netizens have encouraged cultural rituals and genres that have become resources for engagement (網絡爭論) and release. Even though sexuality and pornography may play a less central role in the typical attitudes of activist groups, they are included in public debates and actions. The cultures of contention have helped people to reclaim their animal instincts (動物本能) and debate the nature of sexual desire as social life. The turn towards sexual expressivity is a way for people to accumulate and share bodily energies while testing the boundaries of government policing.

Theorists of network society have pointed out that cultural movements can spread like contagious viruses (傳染性病毒). Government authorities are increasingly threatened by the swarm-like nature of these movements and in some instances try to launch a counter-epidemic (Sampson 2009). The ability to move and act together like a buzzing entity creates a space free from individual persecution. For example, a Shanghai-based blogger suggested that online statements that might be considered dissident should be labeled "Wang". In this

Figure 8: Image which accompanied the "Declaration of Anonymous Citizens" action against censorship, 2009.

way they would adopt the most common Chinese name in order to spread information and opinion to the masses while humorously circumventing keyword-driven government censorship.

This strategy of anonymity was taken up in the 2009 "Declaration of Anomymous Netizens" (匿名網民宣言) that was posted on the website Global Voices Online in response to the government's attempt to impose the Green Dam Youth Escort filtering software. As the netizens wrote:

> We take no interest whatsoever in your archaic view of state power and your stale ideological teachings. You do not understand how your grand narrative dissipated in the face of Internetization. We are the sum of the world's entire online population. We are omnipresent … We are an army. We do not forgive. We do not forget. (Lam 2009a)

Matteo Pasquinelli analyzes the power dynamics of the open Internet culture in his book *Animal Spirits: A bestiary of the Commons*. Based on Virno's philosophy of the multitude

(民眾/人群), Pasquinelli introduces the concept of "immaterial civil war" where the "open animals of the world" combine creative talents to reveal internalized power structures. Pasquinelli makes reference to an old Jewish-Dutch proverb, "The greater the spirit, the greater the beast," to suggest a dialogic structure that would be present in innovative or radical web culture. As he writes: "At the level of base energies, aggressiveness, innovation and revolution all share the same wellspring – the same obscure source that feeds state power as well"(Pasquinelli 2009: 30). The traditional enemy lines between the repressive nation-state and the voices of activism becomes blurred, as each makes use of popular emblems to adopt unique strategies of inspection and intimidation.

Chinese activists have adopted an eroticization of animal spirits to help in the fight against government censorship. For instance, the peculiar animal "Grass Mud Horse," (草泥馬) became an Internet meme in 2009 and was widely used as a defiant symbol that counteracted widespread Internet censorship. Ten mythical animals were created on the interactive encyclopedia Baidu Baike and people started using them as a mode of humorous, vulgar protest. Amongst the other animals were the "French-Croatian Squid" ('Fuck you', 法克,鱿 fa ke you), the "Small Elegant Butterfly" (original Japnese: 止めて [yamete], to stop 雅蠛蝶, ya mie die) and the "Chrysanthemum Silkworms" (菊花蠶, originally 菊花残,

Figure 9: The mythical animals "Grass Mud Horse" and "Small Elegant Butterfly" were invented in a fight against the government decision to have all PC's installed with the anti-pornography filtering software Green Dam Youth Escort.

Figure 10: Grass Mud Horse is merged together with a giant robotic character. It is portrayed as a powerful and sexual furry animal that runs around, tramples and destroys its environment.

Chrysanthemums scattered). All of these Chinese names can also vaguely refer to Chinese profanities, as they utilize homophones and characters whose meaning changes when a different tone is applied.

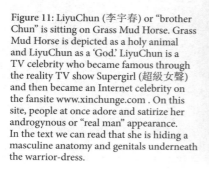

Figure 11: LiyuChun (李宇春) or "brother Chun" is sitting on Grass Mud Horse. Grass Mud Horse is depicted as a holy animal and LiyuChun as a 'God.' LiyuChun is a TV celebrity who became famous through the reality TV show Supergirl (超級女聲) and then became an Internet celebrity on the fansite www.xinchunge.com . On this site, people at once adore and satirize her androgynous or "real man" appearance. In the text we can read that she is hiding a masculine anatomy and genitals underneath the warrior-dress.

Figure 12: The character in green outfit is called Lady Green Dam (綠壩娘). Like Grass Mud Horse, she was invented by people to criticize the government proposal to install the filtering software Green Dam Youth Escort on all PC computers. In this cartoon, she parades in her green uniform and warns people not to watch Hentai erotica. Meanwhile she herself gets sucked into the screen. She has written a slogan on her blackboard that says: "Harmonize Your family" (河蟹你全家).

The Grass Mud Horse is supposedly a species of the alpaca. The name is derived from cào nǐ mā (肏你妈), whose near-equivalent word translates as "fuck your mother". The greatest enemy of the Grass Mud Horse is the "river crab" (河蟹) whose name resembles 和谐 héxié meaning "harmony", referring to government censors who wish to create a "harmonious society."(和諧社會, hexie shehui) (Lam 2009b). The Grass Mud Horse spurred people's imagination, as was evidenced in the thousands of image-collages and mockumentaries that have appeared online. The fad spread like a benign virus and was later popularized as a stuffed animal, an activist icon-turned commodity. The popular theme song of the Grass Mud Horse was banned by The State Administration of Radio, Film, and Television in March 2009 together with the official blocking of the entire meme itself. The mythic figure survived and was later creatively conjoined with "Green Dam Girl" (綠壩娘) a satirical cartoon character who protects state interests. She preaches a compulsive rhetoric of "harmonizing the family," acting like a bossy government official who enjoys saddling people with moral directives. The surreal and humorous qualities of these figures tapped into a populist stream, or indeed pop culture itself, and helped to spur a viral movement of protest.

Artists and writers have contributed to debates about open Internet culture through creative acts of protest or by uploading their own representations of the body and its sex appeal. In literature there has been a cultural uproar around the genre of "hookers' literature" (妓女文學) or "pretty girl literature" (美女文學). This is a genre of mostly general women's fictional erotic writings, sometimes "written with the lower body." One famous author is Jiu Dan (九丹) who in 2001 published her famous novel *Crow* (烏鴉), which was based on her experiences as a student in Singapore, where she and other Chinese women became sex workers in order to survive financially and to secure a Visa or residency permit. Her novel uses the crow as a metaphor to describe the living conditions of women who collectively fly to advanced countries and sell their bodies for sex. Jiu Dan was vigorously attacked by her readers, some of whom accused her of cheap sensationalism and ruining the image of Chinese women worldwide.

Other artists have made use of photography to cast and frame their naked bodies as vehicles for hedonistic pleasure and sexual entertainment. In Hong Kong in 2008, artist and Internet celebrity Siu Ding (小丁) started uploading cunning naked self-portraits. She reached full digital fame when she performed in the nude for a music video by the local indie band Forever Tarkovsky Club. In their video entitled "Half-Naked Christmas Party" (聖誕半裸派對), dressed as a Japanese school girl, Siu Ding ran around the lush countryside of Sai Kung while slowly taking off her clothes. The announcement of the launch party for this video was misinterpreted by a Hong Kong journalist who forwarded it to the police, thinking the band would be organizing an actual Christmas-day orgy. After the closing down of the party, and it appearing in the news, web users tracked down Siu Ding's personal blog and photos, and reposted them on popular forums (Wong 2009). Siu Ding regrets the fact that the news was blown out of proportion by the local newspapers, *Oriental Daily* (東方日報) and *Apple Daily* (蘋果日報), some of whose reportage zoomed in only on her naked appearance while ignoring the band who had organized the event. Nevertheless, she

Figure 13: Hong Kong artist and Internet legend Siu Ding frequently uploads nude images on her blog www.siuding.com and the social network facebook in order to reclaim the naked female body. Photographs by Suckphoto.

Figure 14: Siu Ding, 22 Morning Street, Lok Wah Tsuen. The artist casts herself as a tiny naked person in front of dehumanizing skyscraper architecture.

became quite familiar with how the mass media exploits sexuality and how mainstream journalists tend to pry into personal information and sensational details.

In some of her Internet uploads and artistic photographs, she uses imaginative modes of self-display to reclaim nudity. She uses a personal blog and the social network Facebook to regularly upload her snapshots and art photos from her domestic sphere, some of which include nudity. While her blog posts survive censorship, her Facebook posts are often instantly deleted by the administrators. In a series of photographs shot by Hong Kong photographer Suckphoto, we see her as a cute and messy girl who likes to smear herself with fluids and foods. She looks confidently into the camera while showing off her petite and naked body in its cozy home environment surrounded by personal objects, foods and her ubiquitous cat.

In the series *22 Morning Street* she is photographed totally nude in front of the many buildings she lived in when starting life as a young adult. She explains that she left her family home at a young age and could only afford to live in shabby places, but they left a deep imprint on her. These naked photos reveal her body as a tiny and almost invisible figure that streaks and poses in front of post-industrial urban sceneries. To gaze at her body means to view a delicate organism finding its way through life and a congested metropolis. Rather

Figure 15: Xu Yong and Yu Na, Solution Scheme, 2009. Yu Na is a former sex worker who collaborated with Xu Yong to reinvent her naked body as an art work. She is at once a sexy courtesan and an artist in control of the process of photography. Her facial expression also radiates cynicism and boredom, while her suitors are generic looking government workers who seem uninterested in her.

than zooming in on the body, the camera zooms out and shows us how the body is almost lost. As Siu Ding explains in an interview: "If I were to be wearing clothes or costumes, people would get distracted and start looking at those elements, so I wanted to keep it very simple. It is about a body looking for a place." Siu Ding's search is too abstract for viewers to become truly aware of it as a force of eroticism. Rather, her portrayal of nudity is a slight but powerful interlude in a landscape of commercialized and sanitized sexual imagery.

Other artists have contributed with cheeky and thought-provoking portrayals of nudity. Yu Na (俞娜) is a mainland Chinese artist and former sex worker who uses her sexuality and prostitute branding in order to transform her body into a vehicle for art. In the series of photographs *Solution Scheme* (解决方案) which she made in collaboration with photographer Xu Yong (徐勇), the artist comments on the inevitable decadence underlying China's newly-found affluence. She functions as the director of scenes where she also appears as the luscious, naked female model. By holding the cable that controls the camera's shutter, the photograph shows that she maintains the dual role of artistic director and model. The viewer can stare at her perfect naked body, which will be captured in just the way she likes it. In the photographs, Yu Na surrounds herself with seemingly-bored, uniformly-dressed men, symbolic cadres of Chinese power elites.

Ellen Pearlman has argued in her paper "Chinese Women: Sexuality and Costume as Power and Individuation" that Yu Na casts herself as confident and dominant female in relation to the men who surround her (Pearlman 2009). For instance, she wears dark glasses that are associated with China's undercover agents, or she carries a flag which can be interpreted as a symbol of male power. However, in my own reading of these photographs, the subversive quality lies in her repetitively-bored facial expressions. She is shown to be a detached and melancholic person. Moreover, Yu Na's gaze deconstructs the binary opposition between the "tops and bottoms" of sex work. Even though she is indeed cast as a sex bomb, she also appears to be sleepy and bored, just like her clients. Both women and men are about to fall asleep while performing a worn-out tribute to their sex drive. The photos convey a mechanical world of socially-engrained rituals.

In her diary accompanying the photographs, Yu Na writes candidly and emotionally about her life as a sex worker and her desire to sleep with many men. The diary is honest and full of life, but also reveals her criticism of commercialized sex culture. Just like their male counterparts, female workers are caught in a cycle of a day-in-day-out entrepreneurialism which, in the scheme of survival, becomes difficult to quit. In this sense, the revelation of her desire to have a traditional relationship that produces a child shows a more complex layering of the personality shown in *Solution Scheme* (Xu Yong and Yu Na 2009).

Conclusion

Chinese activists and artists use various tactics to comment on a changing sex culture within the advanced social networks and policing mechanisms of surveillance society.

They employ satirical strategies and differing forms of sexual documentary to protect and release the sexual body while also commenting on the Chinese Internet crisis. While the CCP government hires and funds web users to post government propaganda and spy on illegal licentious activities, people are able to develop resistant identities and continue their search for illicit pleasures and novel sexualities. In this respect there has been a growing rift between government-supported attitudes about pornography and people's actual thoughts and practices.

Despite waves of cynicism and despair about nation-state censorship, people continue to build and share their hacked and DIY collections. Sometimes people document each other's private affairs malignantly and moralistically, or against the will of the involved parties. Other times, the making and circulating of DIY sex materials are shown to be part of joyful and consensual activities. Aside from being immersed in pornography as a creative outlet and sexual release, people develop tropes of satire and subversive icons in order to comment on sexuality. One famous example is the online circulation of the surreal figure of the Grass Mud Horse, a satirical emblem and Internet meme used to criticize authoritarian power. Hordes of netizens made their own versions of this strange alpaca species, whose name also sounds like a nasty swear word. The Grass Mud Horse can be seen as the anonymous and strategic adoption of an awkward animal spirit that nevertheless stands up against government and its compulsive and paradoxical demand for a harmonious society.

New forms of sexual entertainment have emerged but their roles in public culture are still carefully controlled by government and the mass media. China's sexual boom is indeed formulated under a patriarchal premise and its engrained binary gender roles. The fantasies show hungry male clients who unleash their repressed desires and are served by youthful and submissive females. But a younger generation of women is more adept at seizing power within burgeoning media industries. There has been a new wave of art and writings from sex workers who have made unusual and unique confessions in order to reclaim their bodies and lifestyles.

Notes

1. The interviews and focus groups for this chapter were conducted at City University of Hong Kong, November 2009, and at Beijing Women's University, February 2010.
2. Information about the movie "Country Uncle" can be found in the following blog posts http://vinta. ws/blog/359 and http://www.tianya.cn/publicforum/content/filmtv/1/190422.shtml (accessed 15 July 2011).
3. The interview with Dr. Li Yinhe, Chinese Academy of Social Sciences, was carried out in 20 March, 2010.
4. Comments about the TV sitcom Woju were compiled from Sina and Douban http://survey.eladies. sina.com.cn/result/39432.html; http://www.douban.com/review/2770528/ (accessed 12 July 2011).

References

Bernstein, Elizabeth (2007) *Temporarily Yours: Intimacy, Authenticity, and the Commerce of Sex,* Chicago: University of Chicago Press.

Chang, Ying (2009) "State Broadcast Television Administration Recalled Wo Ju for a Second Trial. The 2.0 Version Shall Be A Purified One," *Xinhuanet,* 1 December, http://www.tj.xinhuanet.com/movieteleplay/2009-12/01/content_18377113.htm (accessed 11 July 2011).

China Digital Times (2009) "China Says 5395 arrested in Pornography Crackdown," *China Digital Times,* (online) 31 December, http://chinadigitaltimes.net/2009/12/china-says-5394-arrested-in-Internet-pornography-crackdown/ (accessed 11 July 2011).

Demick, Barbara (2010) "Paranoia the Best Censor," *South China Morning Post,* 24 April.

Han Han (2010a) "Google in China," *China Digital Times,* (online) 15 January, translated by Anne Anna, http://chinadigitaltimes.net/2010/01/han-han-speaks-out-on-google-in-china/ (accessed 11 July 2011).

Han Han (2010b) "From Now On, I am a Vulgar Person," *China Digital Times,* (online) 22 January, translated by China Geeks, http://chinadigitaltimes.net/2010/01/han-han-%E2%80%9Cfrom-now-on-i%E2%80%99m-a-vulgar-person%E2%80%9D/ (accessed 15 may 2010).

He, Qinglian (2008) *The Fog of Censorship: Media Control in China,* New York: Human Rights in China.

Henan People Daily (2009) "China Youth Daily: Zhoukou City Serves and Guides the Youth in Creating a New Internet Space," November 30, http://henan.people.com.cn/news/2009/11/30/437919.html Translated on *China Digital Times* http://chinadigitaltimes.net/china/Internet-commentators (accessed 11 July 2011).

Lam, Oiwan (2009a) "Declaration of Anonymous Netizens," *Global Voices Online,* 24 June, http://advocacy.globalvoicesonline.org/2009/06/24/china-2009-declaration-of-the-anonymous-netizens (accessed 17 July 2011).

Lam, Oiwan (2009b) "Good Bye Grass Mud Horse," *Global Voices Online,* 18 March, http://globalvoicesonline.org/2009/03/18/china-goodbye-grass-mud-horse/ (accessed 13 July 2011).

Lim, Gerrie (2007) "The State of Asian Pornography," In *Asian Sex Gazette,* (online) 1 July, originally published in AVN.online.com and reprinted with permission, http://www.asiansexgazette.com/asg/southeast_asia/southeast08news76.htm (accessed 11 July, 2011) .

Lim, Gerrie (2004) *Invisible Trade: High-Class Sex for Sale in Singapore,* Singapore: Monsoon Books.

Lyon, David (2007) *Surveillance Studies: An Overview,* Malden MA: Polity Press.

Ottomo, Massimo (2010) "A Field Guide to Sola Aoi, The Pornography Star who Brought Down China's Great Firewall," 22 April, http://fleshbot.com/5522012/a-field-guide-to-sola-aoi-the-pornographystar-who-brought-down-chinas-great-firewall (accessed 13 July 2011)

Pasquinelli, Matteo (2009) *Animal Spirits: A Bestiary of the Commons,* Rotterdam: Nai Publishers.

Parish, William L., Lauman, Edward O. and Mojola, Sanyu A. (2007) 'Sexual Behavior in China: Trends and Comparisons," *Population and Development Review,* 33: 4, pp. 729–56.

Pearlman, Ellen (2009) "Chinese Women: Sexuality and Costume as Power and Individuation," Paper presented at *Extra/Ordinary Dresscode: Costuming and the Second Skin in Asia* Conference, City University of Hong Kong, November.

Sampson, Tony (2009) "How Networks Become Viral," in *The Spambook: On Viruses, Pornography, and Other Anomalies from the Dark Side of Digital Culture* New Jersey: Hampton Press, (pp. 39–61).

Siuming, Pan (2006) "Transformations in the Primary Life Cycle: the Origins and Nature of China's Sexual Revolution," in E. Jeffreys (ed) *Sex and Sexuality in China,* New York: Routledge.

Times of India (2009) "China Pays Surfers To Find Pornography," *The Times of India* (online), 7 December, http://chinadigitaltimes.net/2009/12/china-pays-web-surfers-to-find-porn/ (accessed 11 July 2011).

Wong,Nicole (2009) "Getting Noticed at Last," *China Daily,* (online) 24 January, http://www.chinadaily.com.cn/hkedition/2009-01/24/content_7426638.htm (accessed 11 July 2011).

Wu, Zhaohui et al. (2010) "A Peep at Pornography Web In China," in *Proceedings of the WebSci10: Extending the Frontiers of Society On-Line,* 26-27th April, Raleigh, NC: US. http://journal.webscience.org/306 (accessed 11 May 2011).

Xie, Qingyun (2010) "China's Anti-Pornography Campaign Starts Green Bookmark Action 2010," *Sing Tao Global Network,* (online) 13 June, http://feature.stnn.cc/news/saohuang/ (accessed 11 July 2011).

Xinhua Agency (2010) "China Issues White Paper on Internet Policy," *China.org* (online), 8 June, http://china.org.cn/china/2010-06/08/content_20206978_3.htm (accessed 11 July 2011).

Xu, Yong and Yu Na (2009) *Solution Scheme,* Hong Kong: Culture of China Publication Co.

Xue Ying (2009) "Green Dam: Chinese Netizens are All Children," *Cn Reviews,* (online)16 June, http://cnreviews.com/life/news-issues/green-dam-chinese-neitzens-children_20090616.html (accessed 11 July 2011).

Yang, Guobin (2010) "Why Google Should Not Quit," *Social Science Research Council Website,* (online) 15 January, http://www.ssrc.org/features/view/why-google-should-not-quit (accessed 11 July 2011).

Yau, H. Y. and Wong H.W. (2009) "The Emergence of a New Sexual Ideal: A Case Study of Yuki Maiko's Pornographic VCDs in Hong Kong," *Journal of Archaeology and Anthropology,* 70 (2009), pp. 1–46.

Yu, Verna (2010) "Chopping Away At the Wall of Injustice," *South China Morning Post,* 5 April.

Zhang, Lifan (2010) "A Confession of an Internet Naked Runner," Translated by Oiwan Lam, In *Global Voices Online,* 5 March, http://globalvoicesonline.org/2010/03/05/china-a-confession-of-an-Internet-naked-runner/ (accessed 11 July 2011).

Zheng, Tiantian (2009) *Red Lights: The Lives of Sex Workers in Postsocialist China,* Minneapolis: University of Minnesota Press.

Chapter 2

The Pride and Pettiness of Sex Bloggers

Introduction

The second chapter highlights the contributions of Chinese bloggers to the burgeoning online sex industries. It analyzes eroticism and political activism amongst digital celebrities and citizen-journalists who widen sex culture beyond the sanctified domains of entertainment and the mass media. Rather than positioning sex bloggers on the road to enlightenment or social liberation, I would argue that they embody a paradoxical sensibility of pride and pettiness within their self-created and emerging domains. It will be shown that bloggers underscore the discrepancy between a sexual renaissance and the state-induced "propaganda of impotence" (宣揚性無能) in the words of Han Han (韓寒). In addition to the quest for civil liberties and public assembly, there has been a growing cult of writers and artists who want to depict their unusual and/or excessive sex lives. These bloggers defend and celebrate bodily passions in the face of sex-phobic impulses and the state-controlled media. At the same time, as shown in the analysis of sex scandals involving online vigilantes, a sensibility of crude voyeurism and mob intolerance (暴民粉絲) has shaped itself around the blogging culture.

Chinese Communism has been transformed by an entrepreneurial capitalism that seeks out novel sex products, yet maintains the criminalization of radical non-conformity and political dissidence (Rofel 2007: 121). One of the bloggers who perhaps most clearly personifies this paradigm was Mu Mu, a young Communist party member and student from an elite university who became famous as an erotic webcam dancer. From her writings we know that her followers were of high class, "bankers", "scholars", "lawyers", and even "a Buddhist abbot." She was the girl who was destined, in her own words, "to bridge the gap between intellectual and sexual merits." She explains that she was glad to be born in the age of market reform and pushed to enjoy new lifestyle options and capitalist concepts of individuality:

I am definitely the dance babe who reads the most and thinks the deepest, and I'm most likely the only party member among them. People argued that I was pursuing Communism with a petite bourgeois attitude. But my college life is just a piece of performance art …

In China, the concepts of private life and public life have emerged only in the past 10 to 20 years. I'm fortunate to live in a transitional society, from a highly political one to a commercial one … and this allows me to enjoy private pleasures, like blogging. (Wilde 2005)

UNIVERSITY OF WINCHESTER
LIBRARY

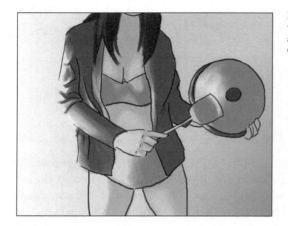

Figure 1: Blogger Mu Mu in one of her anonymous webcam dances. Mu Mu never revealed her face and wrote about her status as an elite student and Communist party member.

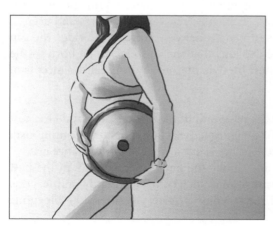

Bloggers wish to expand their erotic spirits into marketable digital lifestyles, but they are subject to stigmatization by the government and their peers in relation to their choice of civic discourse and sexual entertainment. The body and its new sexual shell are fragile entities that are easily threatened and possibly demolished by the agents of Chinese surveillance society.

People's Artists with Virtues and Professional Skills

In April 2010, the Chinese State Council published its White Paper on Internet Policy (網絡白皮書), which stated that there are 220 million bloggers in China and that 66 per cent of Internet users actively partake in civic debate, which would result in 3 million messages daily (Xinhua Agency 2010). The glitzy statistics of the White Paper were immediately challenged by Internet activist Isaac Mao Xianghui (毛向輝), research fellow at Harvard University's Berkman Centre for Internet and Society in 2010, who stated that the total of daily messages should have been around 76 million rather than 3 million. In his counter-report about China's White Paper, which was published in the *South China Morning Post*, Mao argued that, in actuality, 95 percent of blogging messages are still censored and deleted on a daily basis. Moreover, censorship mechanisms are tightening and have shifted from the removal of specific content and sensitive keywords to entire websites and social networks (Nip 2010).

Since 2002 Mao himself has been one of China's pioneering bloggers, in addition to being a social entrepreneur, philosopher of "sharism," (or cultural zones of sharing), and a software architect in social technologies. His bold response to the White Paper shows that radical blogging is still a chancy mission in China, as dissident statements are read and deleted by the armies of surveillance. In the same vein, even though some of these bloggers meet and organize publicly through an annual Chinese Blogger Conference (entitled CNBloggerCon), they have to be careful in publicizing the details of these conferences in order to avoid from the scrutiny of the police.

In a talk about his life as a pioneering blogger, Mao argues for a new individualism (全新的個人主義世界觀) that can help people stand out and step away from a long tradition of collectivism:

> China has a long tradition of people trying to fit into the group, moderating their behavior to avoid standing out conspicuously – a culture reinforced by the man-made collectivism of the past half-century. Blogs have leapfrogged this tradition, acting as a catalyst to encourage young people to become more individual. So this and other grassroots media are now emerging strongly to challenge China's social legacy. (Schokora 2008)

Discussions amongst bloggers also have helped create an atmosphere of intelligent feedback and tolerance. Even though there is still an urge to partake in collectivist "good behavior" and/or harassment of "others," netizens have come to defend the values of non-standardized lifestyle choices and the diversification of thought.

As will be shown in this chapter, Mao's "leapfrog" has been taken up by activists and sex bloggers alike. For instance, February Girl (二月丫頭) was one of the most outspoken sex bloggers to support individualism and self-imaging in a quest to rediscover a Chinese erotic heritage. As she argued elegantly in one of her essays about the female body:

> I am a woman whose biggest shortcoming is that I am determined to do what I like. I don't care what others think. I do things which I consider right and harmless. Since I am holding an exhibition of my body, I have to do it right and take it seriously. In order to make better pictures, I tried hard to find my summer dresses and wear them in the February wind. Yes indeed, those pictures with my lovable breasts are made with great efforts.
>
> Speaking of the Chinese tradition of being restrained, I would have to date that back to a long, long time ago. Our ancestors had their fertility cults. They painted and carved the shapes of genital organs. Or how about the naked fashion we see in the Dunhuang mural paintings? I think all of you know about those, right? And also, the literature about the beauty of nakedness, you know that too, don't you? I will tell you something – back then naked dancing was pretty popular. Are you having a hard time listening to me now? And then it was Tang Dynasty, when women dressed down much more than me. Revealing boobs was just common. It is said that the low-cut dress actually originated in China. (February Girl 2006)

The self-portraits of February Girl were simple and subdued, but her proud attitude was cherished and commented upon by netizen mobs. She was one of the many bloggers who confidently turned individual outbursts and creative flows into a public consensus built around sexuality. She paved the way for the more radical "body artists" like Su Zizi (蘇紫紫), a student at Renmin University who, in 2011, confidently displayed her naked body inside a fish tank. Su Zizi argued that public nudity is one way for her to advance artistically and economically, as she grew up in economic and emotional hardship in Hubei Province and was abused by her father (Li Hao 2011). Su Zizi titillated journalists, while openly expressing her victim status and need to create a radical performance statement out of it. Like her predecessors, she offered a kind of sexual entertainment and criticism that is largely absent in the official curriculum of state-endorsed schools and media institutions.

The new individualism is also typified in the public support for overseas porn stars who offer their own type of sexual expressivity and sex education. Chinese netizens admit to craving contact with Japanese AV stars. For instance, the Japanese porn star Sola Aoi (蒼井空) became a celebrity in mainland China through her heavy activity on Twitter. She is a self-proclaimed geekgirl who enjoys hyper blogging on Twitter and its Chinese twin site, Weibo (微博), reporting on daily life and promoting her work. She purports to writing all these micro-posts herself and responds personally and eagerly to her army of followers. She mostly blogs about daily trivia such as food, shopping and fashions but also makes sure to pay her dues to foreign fans.

Figure 2: Blogger February Girl and the cleavage that made her famous. February Girl wrote about the beauty of female bodies and defended the notion of a Chinese erotic heritage. Digital Drawing by Bonni Rambatan.

Figure 3: Screenshot of the blog of Japanese AV actress Sola Aoi, who became an Internet legend and micro-blogger in China through her activity on Twitter and Weibo.

Figure 4: Sola Aoi Publicity Photo.

One could think of Sola as the ideal porn star for China as she fits one of the physical ideal types of "baby face with large breasts"(童顏巨乳). In one of Sola's widely-watched video clips on Youtube.com, she bobs around on a bed like a silly little girl who stares into the camera and teases the curious viewer. At age 24, she is also a seasoned entrepreneur who travels the world and aims at becoming a star beyond the world of AV.

Sola attracted about 20,000 followers on the first day of setting up her Twitter account on April 11, 2010. Many of them were mainland Chinese men who managed to "Jump the Great Fire Wall" (翻牆), and thus illegally accessing the banned site. Sola started to interact with her Chinese followers and commented on various aspects of their Chinese culture and the news, such as her love for authentic Chinese cuisine, the Shanghai World Expo (上海世博會) or the Qinghai earthquake of April 2010 (青海地震). On 15 April 2010, she published an auto-translated open letter to her Chinese fans: "Thank you, my breast lovers in China." On 26th April, 2010, she announced on her blog a fund-raising campaign for the Qinghai Earthquake victims. She wrote that she strongly empathized with earthquake victims because she was born and raised in a country where earthquakes happen very frequently. Her message went viral on the Chinese Internet and she officially launched her campaigns by selling self-photographed pictures.

Figure 5: Sola Aoi posts image of her freshly-painted fingernails on her blog.

Her earthquake campaign was a huge hit in China. She managed to raise 200,000 yen within a couple of weeks, which won her the nickname of "People's Artist with both Virtues and Professional Skills" (Fei 2010). She gave the money to the Japanese Red Cross, who then transferred it to the Chinese Red Cross. [1]

At the time of the Qinghai earthquake in 2010, her Chinese fans commented that not only did she have a beautiful body, but also a beautiful soul. Several months later, Sola made a promotional trip to Shanghai as part of a televised online game distribution ceremony. Sola was to be featured with two other Chinese digital celebrities – the bloggers Sister Phoenix (鳳姐) and Sister Lotus (芙蓉姐姐). Chinese netizens wrote that it was humiliating that Sister Sola would be featured together with the two Chinese "media tarts." Sister Phoenix and Sister Lotus had previously been widely attacked as opportunistic media whores who generally lacked talent. Sister Phoenix revealed herself as a ruthless gold digger when she was caught handing out flyers near her university stating that she was looking for a husband with a global vision and a finance degree from Peking University or Qinghua University (Quartly 2010). Sister Lotus became an Internet legend after uploading vain self-photography accompanied by essays concerning life and love. She was widely lambasted for being ugly, overweight and self-absorbed. When a TV program devoted to her was pulled from the

Figure 6: Sister Lotus became famous for her S-shaped signature dance and writing essays about love. She was widely disliked for being overweight and vain.

Figure 7: Cartoon about Sister Phoenix who became famous for being an overly-demanding material girl who publicized her exact requirements when dating men.

air, she fought back and defended free speech by acting out a specific type of contortionist signature dance that supposedly explained her views and her ambitions (Cody 2005).

It was clear from audience reactions during the game distribution ceremony that Sister Sola, or "Teacher Sola," as she was nicknamed by some of her most devoted fans, was considered to be of higher rank than the two Chinese celebrities. After her talk show appearance, she tweeted that "It was great that I could perform on the same stage with those two Chinese Internet icons, but their looks were a little weird." One of her disciples Qianhao19860810 shot back: "They are indeed Chinese local specialties. Hope Sister Sola was not too bothered."

But why would it be the case that a Japanese porn star became so highly respected by Chinese fans, while the Chinese sexpert are constructed in a negative vein? In my view, Sola is not only a good-looking petite with an ample bosom, she is also a hyper communicative tri-lingual free netizen who represents the New World Dream (新世紀夢想). She is a cosmopolitan go-getter who offers a new brand of viral marketing and online entertainment. She knows how to play the Chinese markets through exotic representations that tap into contemporary transnational trends in sexuality. She is also fortunate enough to be able to illegally sell her products in China despite harsh censorship rules applicable to local citizens.

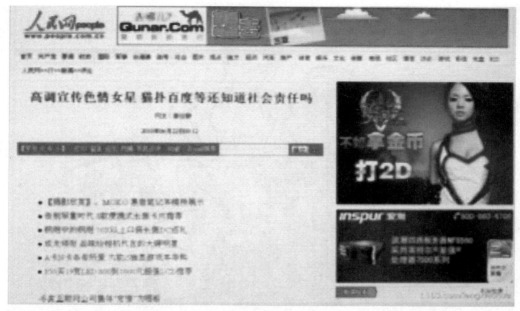

Figure 8: Advertisement in People.com for Sola Aoi TV appearance, next to an article denouncing her popularity.

Sola Aoi was further praised on the entertainment portals Mop.com and Baidu.com but later these portals were criticized by People.com for being so passionate about a porn star. People.com argued that a pornstar should not be praised, while at the same time a big colorful Sola Aoi advertisement for the televised game promotion was placed directly next to the article condemning her. This incident shows once again that there is paradoxical mindset supporting, on the one hand, sex-phobic dogmatism and, on the other hand, the new entrepreneurial mindset.

It also shows that, despite the official dogma of collectivism and sexual conservatism, China nurtures its digital legends and reaches out for their sexual advice, input, and lifestyle. These waves of digital fame may eventually help the cause of sexual freedom, as women may more publicly embrace the lifestyles and professions associated with sexual entertainment.

Pride and Pettiness: The Janus Face of Internet Fame

Even though a new line of blogging celebrities have taken up the noble cause of sexual liberation, their work consistently elicits large-scale attacks. Statements in favor of joyful vulgarity are easily censored or blown out of proportion by the prying inclinations of moralistic netizens. Often, these attacks implicitly or overtly favor patriarchy, as if female

Figure 9: Hedgehog Mu Mu destabilized the event *Pretty Bloggers* by sending her nude picture to the competition.

sexual agency can only be appreciated if it maintains a pleasant, subdued and non-confrontational attitude.

This is one of the reasons behind the success of the Japanese star Sola Aoi, who in most of her movies embodies the submissive female pose. On top of that, it is also safer and easier for an overseas legend like Aoi to embody a lustful persona, while local Chinese women would be more easily chastised if maintaining similar public profiles. If Chinese women decide to share or upload images of their naked bodies, the negative comments are often staggering. For instance, in 2005, the city of Beijing organized an online beauty pageant, Pretty Bloggers (美女博客), which encouraged female bloggers to upload a selection of their most beautiful photographs and then participate in a beauty pageant. Citizens were encouraged to vote on "the most beautiful blogger" who would win a hefty cash award of 2500 RMB (280 USD). The jury received about 300 submissions from bloggers in various poses and fetching outfits, including one from Hedgehog Mu Mu (刺猬穆穆), who sent in a photograph of herself in the semi-nude. Hedgehog Mu Mu won over a large portion of the three million voters but, in the end, only made it to the top twenty and was also officially reprimanded because of her "lewd" behavior. She also received negative reviews throughout the Internet as netizens argued that she offended the dignity of women (Burns 2006).

Thus, netizens easily revert to petty moral norms when bloggers want to show off their sexual pride. But these attacks are not restricted to instances of female exhibitionism as many public presentations of nudity are condemned on a regular basis. Chinese netizens also tend to attack people's DIY collections and even go as far as illegally stealing them and uploading without their consent. For instance, a famous sex diary and sex tape scandal was that of Wang Cheng (安徽贪官), Director of the Radiation Department of a hospital in Anqing City, Anhui Province (Jiang 2010). The headlines distilled from his diaries point to a quantitative macho impulse: "I plan to have sex with at least 56 women in 2003, 2 of which shall be housewives … The ultimate goal to reach is 600–800 women." His wife found his sex diaries and tapes and a friend of his wife then reported them to the police. At the same time they had been leaked on the Internet by an anonymous party. Even though the government tried to stop this leak, the photographs and videos became some of the most desired items on various Internet forums.

China abounds with such sex scandals and attendant attempts at suppression but lacks proper legislation to protect people's privacy or to support alternative lifestyles. There have been instances of sex-tape or laptop scandals involving beleaguered celebrities in differing Asian cultures, and they almost always trigger reactions of extreme conservatism and revenge. One of these scandals in 2008 involved Hong Kong celebrity Edison Chen, whose case will be further discussed in Chapter 3. A more recent case happened in June 2010, when one of Indonesia's best-known pop singers, Nazril Irham or "Ariel," was detained for breaking the Indonesian anti-porn law by videotaping "promiscuous sex" with two female TV personalities. The sex tapes of the "Peterporn scandal" ("Peterpan" being the name of his band) were widely broadcast on the Internet after being uploaded by one his collaborators, who had obtained them from Ariel's laptop. Instead of persecuting this theft, Irham himself was charged and jailed under the 2008 anti-porn law which makes it illegally to simply film any type of sex act. After the scandal broke, Indonesian Islamic fundamentalist groups rallied in Central Jakarta demanding that Irham be caned and then stoned to death (Agence France-Presse 2010). In addition, the Indonesian Child Protection Commission (KPAI) asked that he publicly apologize for his actions to a fan base of millions of young children.

But, as shown by Singaporean columnist John McBeth, recent statistics show that Indonesia is as much affected by modern search-engine behavior and requests for sex and Internet pornography as any other nation state (McBeth 2010). McBeth goes on to argue that this hypocritical approach to sexuality sends a very somber and discouraging message to the emerging DIY sex cultures. Taiwanese sex activist Josephine Ho agrees that that Asian cybercultures are increasingly falling prone to extreme attitudes of pettiness and intolerance (Ho 2010). The big brother gaze has become internalized as individuals develop anonymous profiles and become self-selected judges in service of their moral crusades. Sometimes, they simply foster desires to secretly-watch private sex lives and expose them to the wider world. This can become a negative impulse with which to project personal anger and frustrations onto sexual crusaders, though netizens will be watching the crusader's journey and downfall like loyal dogs.

Sexual Libertines and the Human Flesh Search Engine

In China there is the related phenomenon of the Human Flesh Search Engine (人肉搜索), in which a group of anonymous netizens collaborate to make up a virtual people's court in order to condemn the suspected individual. They work together, investigating people's personal details, stalking and spying on them, harassing them in both the virtual and physical world. The victims of the Human Flesh Search Engine have included many types of "suspect individuals," from outspoken sex bloggers to corrupt government officials, and multiple others, such as a man who had mischievously uploaded doctored photographs of a new tiger species, or a woman who was photographed while stepping on little kitten with her high stiletto heels.

To a large degree, the Human Flesh Search Engine internalizes repressive state mechanisms and engages in a bullying mentality against perceived (sex) criminals. In December 2008, a woman who had been blogging about her husband Wang Fei and his alleged sex affair, committed suicide. Her death prompted an outpouring of hate mail and physical threats against Wang Fei, instigated via the web. Another example of this web mob mentality came in August 2009 when netizens launched a manhunt for the Shanghai-based ‹Chinabounder›, a mysterious person of Caucasian origin who had sparked fury by boasting of his varied carnal encounters with Chinese women on his blog, "Sex and Shanghai" (Jones 2007). A massive backlash occurred and 17,000 netizens formed a Human Flesh Search Engine, which led to threats of murder and castration from those who claimed the "Sex and Shanghai" blogger had blackened China's good name. It was eventually revealed that this blogger was supposedly a British citizen and Oxford graduate named David Marriot who was writing a book about China's political weaknesses (Telegraph 2008). The vigilantism against Chinabounder had been instigated by Zhang Jiehai (張傑海), a professor of psychology at the Shanghai Academy of Social Sciences (上海社科院). Zhang Jiehai called on web users to "chase down the foreign scoundrel. We must find this foreign filth and kick him out of China." In China's Human Flesh Search Engine mentality, even a psychology professor became paradoxically embroiled in the hate speech directed against a virtually-condemned individual.

In March 2010, another Human Search Flesh Engine invaded the Internet in response to the sex diary by Han Feng (韓峰性愛日記), Head of the Tobacco Department of Laibin City, Jiangxi Province. The diary was uploaded by netizen "han xian zi" on Tianya.cn, the most popular forum in China. The netizen later said that he was the husband of one of Han's lovers. Han Feng's diary was further disseminated online, which led to his dismissal from his official position and later to a jail sentence of 13 years.

Despite being hounded and then condemned by the mobs, Han Feng's diary reveals a fairly benign and reflective sexual crusader. His interweaving of personal sex statistics with the work duties of a Communist official gives a peculiar kind of surreal atmosphere to the confessional diary, as noted in the following entries:

November 6th, Tuesday 11–25°C Sunny

I prepared for the "politeness and courtesy" lecture in the morning. At noon, I accompanied Li Dehui, who came from Xiamen, to have lunch and some wine. I stayed in the dormitory in the afternoon. At night, I had dinner with Huang Huiting and others and I drank quite some wine. Huang and his people are going to Chongqing and Chengdu tomorrow. I will send Su and Tan Shanfang to see them off. At 10ish, Tan Shanfang drove me over to her house. I made love for 3 times. We had one more session early in the morning. I did not ejaculate.

Han Feng admits that he is at once empowered and weakened by his extraordinary lifestyle, as he admits here:

December 4th, Tuesday, 7–23°C, sunny

In the morning I stay in bed. At noon, Zhao Xin, who is from the Qinzhou Court came to deal with some business in the court here. He invited me to lunch and I asked Pan to come with me. We drank till 4ish. I was a little drunk and so was Pan. I asked to her to come to my room and I had sex with her. I remembered it was fierce. She's starting to guide me. There's a lot of love fluid. Pan and Mei invited me to midnight snack, and we invited Qin Gang and myself drank 2 bottles of western wine. I was drunk again.

May 5th Wed 13–22°C, Cloudy
The sex with Pan was too fierce. My whole body was sore and in pain. I stayed in the dormitory the whole day.

Of course these diary entries shed light on the decadent lifestyles of Chinese Communist officials, but the collective impulse to attack their sexual escapades also points to netizen frustration and moralistic regression. These types of intrusion do not reveal a true concern with social change. Even if the diary reveals aspects of social injustice within Chinese culture, the Human Flesh Search Engine has drastic consequences and will rarely motivate itself to operate outside the boundaries of blind revenge.[2]

In contrast to these angry netizen mobs, bloggers with a certain name and profile have managed to make individualized statements about these controversies. For instance, celebrity blogger Han Han published some satirical remarks about the famous Hang Feng diary and then praised the tobacco chief (Zhai 2009: 73). Even though Han Han's tone is typically witty and ironic, he argues that Hang Feng is only a small potato within a larger corrupt system. Han Han writes that Heng Feng is the "least corrupt" of Communist officers, whose first person literature is "refreshing" in an age flooded with generic pornographic pictures and videos. In short, Han Han makes fun of the diary scandal but concludes that people should leave these cases alone and focus on the more serious cases of corruption. I will further elucidate how Han Han aother bloggers use sex discourses in constructive ways to educate people and to posit critical ideas about an authoritarian propaganda of impotence.

Blogging In the Eye of the Hurricane

Despite the fact that websites in China exist under an official ban on sexually explicit images which also leads to sexually explicit language being deleted, both sex bloggers and activist bloggers contribute to a new sexual individualism in defense of pornography and alternative lifestyles. Perhaps the most famous of these activists is Ai Wei Wei (艾未未), an international celebrity artist and fervent social commentator who became a leading public figure when he started criticizing government policies in response to the Sichuan earthquake of 2008. He documented, with the help of a team of researchers, the names of about five thousand students who had perished when poorly-constructed school buildings collapsed during the earthquake. By commenting on ongoing political mishaps and the Chinese propaganda machine, Ai Wei Wei openly criticized the PRC government. He became a widely-respected celebrity, a voice of inspiration and courage for disenchanted youth and netizens, while gradually being a target for repression and criminalization.

And indeed, on 3 April 2011, Ai Wei Wei was detained at Beijing airport and disappeared without any further notice to his wife and family. The lack of legal procedures around his detainment and the official state rhetoric about his supposed misdemeanors caused much panic concerning his well-being. On May 21 2011, 45 days after his detention, it was announced that he would be tried for "tax evasion and deliberately destroying evidence" (Shi 2011). There were reactions of anger and desperation amongst his fanbase and the larger pro-democracy groups in the greater China region. Many in the pro-democracy camp started using photos of Ai's face as their profle picture on Flickr and Facebook. These "Ai faces" were a collective statement of dissidence and a way to identify with the pro-democracy movement. The Ai faces were also creatively and strategically used in street demonstrations in Hong Kong. It was a way for people to "hide their true faces" while impersonating rebellion and "becoming-Ai" – a larger-than-life figure who could maintain a stance of integrity amongst political turmoil.

Other concerned netizens openly deconstructed strategies of government repression, like blogger Love Ai-Love Aiweiwei who devoted his time compiling media coverage about the "rare bird of freedom." [3] This blogger exposed the influence of pro-government bloggers – the infamous "50 Cents Army" (五毛黨), or netizens who are paid by the CCP government to troll online and post comments. He believed that the 50 Cents Army, were inciting people against Ai Wei Wei, as he wrote: "They are indeed everywhere" (Blog, Love Ai-Love Ai Wei Wei 2011). He compiled a list of their inscrutable names and profiles – sd78hgm 67hhl, cxxxgg778, etc. He also stated that Time Magazine's 2011 "Poll for Most Influential Person" was most likely infiltrated by the 50 Cents Army as 10,000 people voted against Ai Wei Wei, which pointed to an orchestrated cyber action. *Love Ai-Love Ai Wei Wei* also showed that he believed that the 50 Cents army were readings his own blog. For example they wrote following comment:

> It is widely known that Ai is a exhibitionist, especially showing his genitals on the Internet so that Internet users can get a chance to be stimulated. Therefore it's not difficult for us to see what a pervert he is, not to add that only his perverted fellow followers are able to appreciate such abnormal behavior.

This comment may appear to be over the top, but actually is in line with one of the official government directives against Ai, whose work does include humorously-naked self-portraits. The first government bulletins against Ai after his disappearance accused him of being an inferior artist who spreads pornographic content. The CCP further argued that eccentric artists like Ai Wei Wei were to be disciplined as they hampered an "overall mission of economic growth and human rights." This point was clearly indicated in the very first state-controlled editorial issued after Ai Wei's Wei's disappearance, entitled "Law Will Not Concede Before Maverick."

> This basic concept of "human rights" has been turned by the West into something that is incompatible with all of the great economic and social advancements of China. This is a great joke. And it is the principal reason why, when the West uses "human rights" to apply pressure on China, it suffers the disdain of the Chinese people . . . The lot of a single Ai Weiwei [sic], and the lots of a few Chinese mavericks (like him), cannot be put on the same level as the development and progress of human rights in China. (Bandurski 2011)

Figure 10: Artist and blogger Ai Wei Wei distributed these images with the Grass Mud Horse to "verify his identity" when opening a new web site. Photocredit Ai Wei Wei.

In May 2009, in order to inaugurate one of his new blogs and "verify his identity," Ai Wei Wei had posted a series of naked photographs. In these photos, he gradually undresses and jumps with joy while holding a stuffed animal version of the Grass Mud Horse in front of his genitals (Schokora 2009). As shown in Chapter 1, the Grass Mud Horse is the humorous, anti-censorship symbol that utilizes a Chinese language double-entendre. It is widely employed by netizens in their ongoing critique of government planning and policy.

In June 1994, Ai Wei Wei had made a reference to the fifth anniversary of the Tiananmen Square massacre. The photograph shows his future wife, Lu Qing, lifting her skirt in front of Mao's portrait in Tiananmen Square. Invoking the famous photograph of Marilyn Monroe standing over subway grating, holding her billowing skirt, Ai Weiwei's mock "tourist" snapshot pointedly suggested an irreverent association between Mao and sex. Moreover, the public space or plaza where political power symbolically resides had been transformed into a shopping plaza, a place where everything, including sex, is for sale. Mao now gazes benevolently on the spectacle of the embrace between a new form of nationalism and the ethos of consumerism (Merewether 2008: 52). One could say that the photograph predicts that China would not be able to develop sexually outside the draw of consumerism nor the visual appeal of erotic imagery.

Figure 11: Ai Wei Wei, June 1994, Photocredit Ai Wei Wei.

But Ai Wei Wei's later career and detention shows that political commentary is at once more stimulating and more dangerous than making art or selling sex as a commodity. As he himself described the power of blogging in China:

Blogging is nothing special abroad, but under China's special social system, blogs have become the most important platform to promote democracy and legal systems, it is a training camp that educates the public and practices civil rights. In the future people will realize the important of this issue. It is our first democratic movement within a civil society. (Ai Wei Wei 2009: 45)

Ai Wei Wei was detained because he contributed to a pro-democracy movement and, as such, was supported by many other bloggers. Zhai Minglei (翟明磊) is pioneering blogger and the editor of the Chinese-language anthology, 《中國猛博：新媒體時代的民間話語力量》 (China's Fierce Blogs: The Power of Civil Discourses in the Age of New Media), including profiles and excerpts of about twenty leading dissident bloggers. Zhai himself used his blogs to criticize the far-reaching practices of Internet censorship and vice squads. For instance, in response to the Green Dam controversies, in which the government wanted to install content-filtering software in all new computers, he wrote that "the government wants to be the father, the teacher and the principle of all behaviors but only wants to make computers for children" (Zhai 2009: 483). He believes that computers are a positive extension of people's sense organs, and that netizens will naturally find online manuals of sex and pornography. He rebuts Communist officials in their willing efforts to sell inferior computers with the pre-installed filtering software:

Honored officers, relax, all your efforts will achieve nothing if you keep selling software of such poor quality. All around us and on our computers, there are still tons of AVs, pornography comics, "in-depth" feet massage houses, street girls, and governors who have second wives. Aren't those sufficient pornography textbooks for the next generation? (Zhai 2009: 483)

Zhai sees the suppression of these "pornography textbooks" as an equivalent to squashing political expressivity: both should be considered very deep, organic and basic human needs.

Since pornography is indeed widely and paradoxically available on Chinese streets and websites, bloggers criticize discourses that officially deny its existence. These official efforts at suppression also highlight a hidden class system in which senior officials easily obtain sexual services while they are tightly controlled when it comes to the ordinary citizens. These instances of elitism combined with sexual decadence has been commented on by blogger Lian Yue (連岳). He developed a satirical Q&A between a foreign journalist and Communist spokesperson. In this text, a spokesperson argues that the legal age of sex with adolescent girls should be dropped from 14 to 4 so that the problem of Communist decadence would be at once erased:

Q: Would you please comment on the vice chief of the Bureau of Meteorology, the party member Chi Quansheng's "buying virgins" incident?

Spokesperson: All levels of officers buy virgins. I have no comment on this.
…

Q: But how can we eliminate similar incidents?

Spokesperson: If this happens again, the government will hand the officer to the public so people can throw stones at him till he's dead.

Q: For real?

Spokesperson: I never tell the truth.

Q: The Criminal Law in your country specifies that having sex with adolescent girls who are under the age of 14 will be classified as rape and the judge should give a heavy penalty. But I don't see these officers being convicted.

Spokesperson: We are going to revise the law into "having sex with adolescent girls who are under the age of 4 will be classified as rape and the judge should give a heavy penalty." There will not be any case of officers raping under-aged girls in the future.

Q: If there's an officer who raped girls under the age of 4, will the revision be a waste?

Spokesperson: At least I can say that revolution is to cross the river by feeling nipples. (Lian Yue 2009: 41)

Another satirical comment on sexual decadence was uploaded by cartoon blogger Li Xiaoguai (李小乖), who calls himself an ordinary person from Foshan city, Guangzhou. He specializes in drawing online comics concerning social upheaval. Xiaoguai became well known, as he draws so fast that his comics come out in response to news he has heard an hour before. In a cartoon entitled "Recycle Bin" he comments on senior official Chen Guanxi, whose recycle bin on his office PC had been found filled with pornographic images.

(Translation of the Cartoon In Praise of the Recycle Bin)

A: Chen Guanxi said in court today that he thought moving files to the recycle bin equaled deleting them. That was why these indecent pictures were found later on his computer.
B: The recycle bin is a great invention indeed!

Figure 12: Cartoon blogger Li Xiaoguai 李小乖, In Praise of the Recycle Bin.

回收站

A: Do you then equally enjoy these kinds of pictures with your people, chief?

B: Nonsense, I never watch that kind of stuff!

A: Then why do you like the recycle bin so much?

B: Last time I made a grave mistake. My appointment to bureau chief by my supervisor was accidentally deleted. Luckily it was just sitting in the recycle bin.[4]

Several other bloggers support the legalization of pornography and recreational sex services. Zhai jokingly writes that he hoped legalization would mean that sex workers would become less pushy and would not keep people awake at night by shouting on the streets. His defense of sex workers is echoed in Luo Yanghuo's (nicknamed "Lao Luo") "Conversations about Prostitutes." Luo founded the famous open blogging platform Bullogger in August 2006, which refuses to use any type of automatic sensitive word filters or other self-censorship systems (Luo 2009: 233). He uses platonic-educational dialogues between himself and his young students about the need to understand and support the shunned profession of sex work.

Lao Hu Miao (老虎廟) or "Tiger Temple," writer of the well-known blog 24 hours online, (24 小時在線博客) is a gonzo journalist who addresses the lives and conditions of laborers as China's "unsung undergrowth" (Zhai 2009: 156). For instance, during the preparations for the Beijing Olympic Games, when most of the of journalists were covering the progress of the magnificent Olympic Stadium, he interviewed homeless peasant workers living outside the walls in shelters made of paper boxes. He reported from their tiny hidden homes about their hardships, ethnic backgrounds and the lack of any social or medical services. As he wrote:

The contractors have built walls that surrounded the whole construction site. They were decorated with Chinese traditional pictures and patterns and they were exquisite to look at. However, behind what looked beautiful was a society of the undercurrents, a group that nobody ever cared about and nobody is willing to care about. From the entrance of walls, I entered the paradise of vagabonds. (Tiger Temple 2009: 161)

Tiger Temple further developed his unique style of blogging when he traveled west from Beijing on a bicycle trip lasting 73 days. On the road, he wrote about the various underground and minority societies that he came across – which he also described as the "bottom of a peacock".

Five days after he started his journey, the Central Propaganda Office released a notice that all news agencies should stop covering his journey. The following warning was issued:

Regarding the Internet blog writer Laohu Miao motorcycling to Shanxi, Inner Mongolia, Shaanxi, Ningxia, and other places to make personal investigation activities and publishing the information online in the name of "grassroots reporting journey," we ask all news organizations not to report on this. In general reports, do not label such acts as "citizen journalism," "civilian journalist" or other equivalent titles. News agencies are requested to strictly comply with order. (Lam and Ip 2009: 39)

Not only were news agencies and journalists required to shun the work of Tiger Temple, but they were also supposed to downplay the development of citizens' journalism itself. Nonetheless, one of his blog posts, about saving an injured dog, aroused people's interests and he finally managed to break down the news blockade.

In tackling the subject of minority rights, Tiger Temple addresses the plight of sex workers, writing in a melancholic tone about their profession while showing that they are part of the fabric of a changing contemporary society. He writes about their seduction rituals at the hotels where he stayed during his trip:

At night, somebody knocked at the door. It was the same soft voice. She asked me what else do I need and brought me a bottle of hot water. She said that if I would write till late at night, I would need tea. I opened the door and thanked her and the hotel for the extraordinary services. She asked me what else do I need again, and again, and she didn't walk away until I said lots of thank-yous. (Tiger Temple 2009: 157)

He encounters sex workers in the most remote towns and villages and learns that they often tumble into this discredited "side business" to make ends meet. As one of his informants, a hotel owner in Inner Mongolia, Erdos City (鄂尔多斯市鄂托克旗框框井), explains:

At first the woman did not have her side business. She was married with a child and she only came out to be a waitress because they could no longer survive. One night, a driver who stayed in our hotel yelled for hot water. He made so much noise at night that nobody could sleep. So I woke up the waitress to boil some water and send the water to him. From that night on, the woman was changed and she began her side business. There are a lot of people doing this in this town and they are all from all over China. There are some who came from the big cities; and others who came from the northeast, Hebei Province, or Hohhot city. There are even some who are from the South. Some are already in their 30s or 40s. They just stand outside to attract customers. The young ones are the most popular ones. They are out of stock at night. Especially on rainy days. Perhaps people are suffering from loneliness and they all thinking of the same thing? (Tiger Temple 2009: 159)

In the next blog post "The Missing Sex Girl" (失踪的春女) the hotel owner is worried because one of the sex workers has disappeared and recent cases of murder easily come to his mind. He asks Tiger Temple if he is equally worried about her and they both hope that the new girl is OK, and has simply run away to a better life.

In recent years, a younger generation of male bloggers has appeared who enchant the masses through their sex appeal and pop-idol status. Many of them are ephemeral and only achieve moments of short-lived fame, but others are more successful in the longer term. The most famous and influential of these bloggers is Han Han, who is also a professional racing driver. Han Han first gained publicity by winning first prize in China's New Concept Writing Competition with his essay, "Seeing Ourselves in a Cup" (杯中窥人), which was about the Chinese national character.

He started his blogging career in an unusual and seemingly dead-end manner having failed seven subjects at the end-of-year examination. He was therefore retained for a year in school. This incident was reported in the media and ignited a heated debate about China's "quality education" (素質教育) policies, and whether holistic or specialized learning should be implemented in schools. Following another seven-subject failure in the senior middle school second year examinations, Han Han finally quit school and soon became a celebrity blogger.

Han Han is most likely China's most widely-read blogger and, potentially, the most famous blogger in the world. He was named "Person of the Year" in 2009 by two influential publications: The Guangzhou-based newspaper *Southern Weekend* (南方周末) and the Hong Kong-based magazine *Asia Weekly* (亞洲周刊) (Xiao 2010). He was also voted as one of a hundred most influential people of 2009 by USA's *Time Magazine*. On 4 June 2010, the eleventh anniversary commemoration of the Tiananmen Square Massacre, CNN Asia Talk interviewed him about his rebel status and political views. He took the occasion to defend the necessity for radical critique of the government:

Even though the Chinese government has improved on the freedom of speech front in recent years, writing is still rather dangerous, so it's quite difficult to strike a balance … But I believe you still need to try despite these difficulties. The situation only improves when there are more people trying; if no one is trying, it only gets more and more difficult. (Cnn.com 2010)

When asked how he can express himself freely without being harassed by the government, he explains that he frames his work as art rather than political dissent. But as some commentators on CNN.com point out, Han Han is still more concerned with his celebrity status and with playing it safe:

> If Han Han would dare to ridicule or criticize the most senior officials, such as President Hu Jintao, he could well end up as a prisoner of Qincheng Prison, a maximum-security prison for dissidents located at the eastern foothills of Yanshan, just northwest of Beijing. But for the time being this remarkable young man can still drive around Beijing in a Bentley. Other writers are less lucky then him. Actually, China has the largest number of imprisoned journalists and authors in the world. "Beautiful birds are the only ones that are caged," as the Chinese say.

When interviewing university students about the popularity of Han Han, they mostly profess adoration and freely defend him, arguing that the government cannot defeat him because he operates "in the eye of the hurricane." He is simply too popular and smart and any government reprisal against him would lead to a serious youth crisis. To these students, blogging is a kind of activity that can host China's new individualism, or the sincere and deeply-critical voices of "beautiful birds." Han Han is indeed a talented and well-poised writer who has a popular power that enables him to steer public opinion.

The original cover of his literary magazine "Duchang Tuan" (独唱团), "Chorus of Solos", has an image of a warrior whose censored genitals are replaced by a gun. In the Chinese language, "defending the center" (挡中央) is a homonym for "the central committee of the Party" (党中央). The image then suggests that the central committee likes to defend its center while depriving it of an actual flesh organ.

As for his contribution to sex and pornography debates, Han Han is more forward than many other bloggers in criticizing a hypocritical attitude about sex. He caused public uproar by openly supporting and linking his blog to the Japanese AV star Kaede Matsushima. He quickly responded to these criticisms by arguing that China is mired in repression and impotency and that, as a new world society, it needs to healthily adapt to adult content. As he writes:

Figure 13: Celebrity blogger Han Han and the original front cover of his magazine, Chorus of Solos, July 2010. The image depicts a satirical image of Central Government.

Our country thinks that these kinds of products are unhealthy. I cannot understand it. If having sex is unhealthy, then we are all unhealthy products. As a matter of fact, this is healthy but our country is not. For any country that has achieved a certain level of economic and cultural growth, sex will be a serious business. If the government insists that it's dirty, obscene, and toxic for youngsters, it only demonstrate that China is still "impotent" and it hasn't stood up in the world …

Japanese AV plays the role of sex enlightenment or sex education lesson for Chinese youngsters. What the youngster should know about any AV movie is that is edited and blown out of proportion for artistic effect. So even if you can not do what the actors do in the movie, you are not impotent. (Han Han 2009: 89)

Han Han is confident about the need to overcome impotence and warns his young followers not to be threatened or overwhelmed by the content of Adult Videos. He himself is of the new sexy males, an online adept, confident and erudite, embodying the cult of individualism as part of a new-world dream. He is more popular and glitzy than the bulk of activist bloggers but, nevertheless, does not compromise the mission of providing quality thought.

Sex Bloggers and The Life of Tiny Arguments

Different from these examples of activists and their sexual commentaries are female bloggers who use the private body as a erotic provocation, employing methods of self-representation and performance art. The Guandong-based blogger Mu Zimei (木子美) could be described as "the mother of Chinese sex blogging," as her explicit online diary was the first one to achieve national notoriety. She openly described her sex life and the various seduction routines that she has used for arranging her one-night stands. She used a specific type of erotic prose-poetry to mimic the clipped, telescopic communication of the one-night stand. Her accounts openly violated traditional morality and conventional notions of gender and love, but they were not politicized in the way that the writings of activists sex bloggers are. Instead of writing about sex and social-political values, she expressed a desire to liberate the "self" or "human nature" from cultural histories and social norms. In short, her blog functioned as a "one-woman liberation movement" centered on a radical defense of sexual pursuits and the ability to separate sex from emotional entanglements. Her blog went viral on the Internet and was taken up by the mass media, who for the most part responded harshly to Mu Zimei's self-styled liberation movement. Yet her media moment became so pervasive that the government finally shut down the "mother blog."

James Farrer carried out a detailed case study of the massive responses that her diary generated in 2003 (Farrer 2007). He did not rely on structured audience-surveys but, rather, sampled and pieced together some of the "social ecology" of love and hatred concerning her personality. He thus registered a "dialogic consciousness" or split ideology about her contribution to sex culture. Blogging is no longer defined in the modes of progress

and backlash but as waves of unresolved and fragmented arguments. Mu Zimei's defense of the lust instinct was, of course, appreciated by her fans and various free-speech proponents, but reactions to her blog had, equally, seeped into much larger critiques of traditional culture. Mu Zimei was a rebel figure who would fight back while maintaining her stance; for instance, she required that journalists sleep with her before granting an interview, using the famous slogan "the longer the sex, the longer the interview" (Farrer 2007).

Professor Li Yinhe of the Bejing Academy of Social Sciences defended Mu Zimei and argued that it was simply her human right to have excessive casual sex and write about it. In her view, Mu Zimei angered people precisely because she challenged the low national sex average:

She actually did not break the law as she did not upload sexually explicit images. She was attacked mainly because people thought that she was too promiscuous, as she slept with so many people. The average sexual partner for each

Figure 14: Mu ZiMei, mother of Chinese sex bloggers who defended libertine values and was widely attacked in 2003.

Chinese person in a life-time is only 1.3, according to our recent statistics. It ranks last but one in the world. So when people saw that she had a lot more than that, they naturally got angry. This kind of anger could be directed at both men and women but it was a worse for her as she was a woman. [5]

Chinese women specifically are discouraged from openly revealing sexual desire as these attitudes are associated with aggression or evil. As Dr. Li explains:

In China, the atmosphere is still that women shouldn't like sex. Men can like sex, and people will just think of them as "lewd". But if women like sex, people will think of them as mean and indecent, or even as evil. Of course women definitely like sex and pornography, I think. A lot of women like it. But they like it less than men, as these social conventions are still quite strong.

Dr Li also believes that Internet bloggers are helping women to seek refuge from social conventions, as these norms are guided by severely-outdated obscenity laws. She explains that, until a decade ago, males and females were getting hefty jail sentences for trying to share home-made sex images. Since sex blogging today includes a distribution of sexually explicit images, the legal consequences could be severe.

February Girl (二月丫頭) is the blogger who became famous by uploading texts and self-photography onto Tianya.com. Photos of her cleavage immediately drew wide attention, though the public's reactions were again intensely negative. Most netizens and the mass media condemned her for being erotic and vulgar, while only a few argued that she was just being brave and candid. Being media-savvy, February Girl knew how to deal with these attacks and fought back with long posts about sexual expressivity:

I posted my own photos in Tianya.cn (天涯社區), one photo after another. There are the ones where I am beautiful, the ones where I am ugly, and the ones where I look cross-eyed and bucktoothed, the ones where I am happy, the ones where I am blue, but in all of them my breasts are exposed.

As a woman, I have the right to show my beauty. I love to see female nudity. I always believe that beautiful things deserve to be appreciated. Unfortunately, the education I received made me unable to convince myself to get totally naked. Moreover, I am not that confident about my beauty, so I don't want to show it all which might hurt your eyes. After serious consideration when putting aside my average face (including my buckteeth) I am still very proud of my huge breasts. (February Girl 2006)

Overall, she argued for women's freedom of exposure but she also condemned casual sex and non-serious relationships. She challenged men about their lack of commitment and inability to please women. She enjoyed a lot of publicity and was interviewed widely in the mass media. Like many of her predecessors, she faded from the Internet with her latest entry dated December 2009.

When I interviewed the more-recently famous sex blogger, Hooligan Swallow (流氓燕), about her interest in pornography she confirmed that it was a difficult topic for her to talk about. But then, like February Girl, she confirmed that pornography could provide a space for sexual rebellion and debate:

> Wow, that is a very private question, but I am glad to share my secrets with strangers, as long as we are not relatives, friends or coworkers. I hope that people who know me won't see these words … When I am in the mood, I will watch Euro-American porn movies to please myself. I think for women in general, we lack opportunities to know more about pornography or how to really get hold of them. However, now things are changing. As women, we have a much broader sexual space, we can learn how to gain sexual pleasure from pornography as well as gain the courage and power to behave in an anti-traditional way.

She adds that the broader sexual space encompasses the use of sexually explicit language and images, which she sees as a basic expression and a basic right. She explains that she cannot exercise this basic right and therefore always needs to invent different words, metaphors and euphemisms:

> People can still understand that I am talking about sex, even though none of my word choices would be perverted or explicit. For instance, during intercourse, if our pubic hair would become curly because we are rubbing against each other, it may look like a women's hairstyle when it is permed. So sometimes when I try to seduce a man, I would say: " Hey let's perm the hair!" (嘿，我們來電發吧)

Other sex bloggers combine sexually explicit images with provocative statements and humor, receiving many hits and comments, as well as attention from supportive international media organs such as the *Asian Sex Gazette*. Blogger Qin Dai (黛秦) created a buzz by posting snapshots of her naked buttocks and back alongside a copy of a romantic novel that she was writing. She responded to negative criticism by comparing her writings to those of Franz Kafka, arguing that being a writer fulfilled her urge to "let her deep-rooted joy and freedom float freely." One of her opponents, Annie Rose, a Kafka connoisseur, attacked Qin Dai, writing, "She can't say how she's like Kafka at all. He was a great writer and had nothing to do with nude ass." She insisted that Qin apologize to her parents and to her buttocks as well.

Yet another trend seeks to gather materials for online archives detailing Chinese people's eroticism; for example, blogger Lost Sparrow was reported compiling an encyclopedia of lovemaking noises based on the premise that they would sound different in different parts of China (Chien 2005). Blogger Hairong Tian Tian (海容天天) collected and posted pictures of men's limp penises. She explained that she wanted, in this way, to explore the "the root of Chinese masculinity" by showing the "cock in its most mundane state" (Skirmisher 2006).

While some sex bloggers made singular and sensationalist or petty media appearances, other have been able to build up a serious and long-term contribution to sexual knowledge and activism. Hooligan Swallow (流氓燕) or "Sister Swallow" (燕姐) is probably the most enduring sex blogger in China. She has managed to continually reinvent herself by establishing blogs and blogging topics related to sexuality. She is currently a fervent poster on Twitter.com with about four thousand followers. She tweets widely about her work, sexual identity, relationships, motherhood, and sex workers' activism. She is a devoted single mother who loves her daughter, tweeting fondly about her:

I look at my little thing asleep with a pillow in her arms. I cannot but kiss her. I am so very happy to be a mother. The little confused bug does not know what is anguish, what is pain, and what is poverty.

Sister Swallow makes clear that she had a rough life as she came from a working class background and always had to fend for herself.

One 4 June 2010 ("July 4" online for censorship purposes) she uploaded a yellow ribbon on her Twitter account which is the network's emblem for Internet freedom. And indeed one can see that she openly and abundantly tackles the sensitive topics of sex work. She believes that sex workers are great role-models as they

… care about men who were abandoned, and give them sexual happiness, comfort, confidence, and even the feeling of being young again.

Her main point is that sex work is such a major trend in society that, at this point, it should be readily accepted. She replies to many of her followers who are concerned that their partners might be seduced by young sex workers. She reassures her concerned followers that many men are still loyal to their wives and sex workers have no desire to threaten relationships:

Sex workers are much less likely to intervene in family matters then a second wife or secret lover, because sex workers have to deal with a lot of males and they do not want to belong to any of these families.

During the time of the 2010 World Cup, she made fun of the Catholic Brazilian soccer player Kaka, who had made a statement against prostitution. She scolded him publicly, telling him to stop preaching and go masturbate:

Kaka, go masturbate! … Those who want prostitutes follow me; those who masturbate follow Kaka! A civil society is one that people have the freedom to choose whether to have sex with prostitutes or masturbate … Anyway, there will be tissue papers everywhere!

Her pioneering sex blog, posted on Tianya.cn. and begun 11 May 2005, had made her famous overnight. She posted a very clear picture of herself half-naked and the next day, she

Figure 15: Catholic Brazilian soccer player Kaka and his stance against prostitution during World Cup 2010.

posted a totally naked picture. Many people responded, attacking her for her looks, arguing that her body did not deserve to be presented in a public space. She struck back with a defense of ordinary bodies:

> I am not rich, but I am determined to enjoy my life as those who can, and be happy as those who are happy. I am not pretty, and my body is not perfect, but the world still belongs to me. I won't give up just because of your condemnation. I live for myself, not your praises.

The Hooligan effect kept growing, engendering condemnation and attempts to humiliate her personality. Traffic on the site became so heavy that it was rumored that Sister Swallow had paralyzed Tianya's traffic. She dealt openly and publicly with all these insults and even

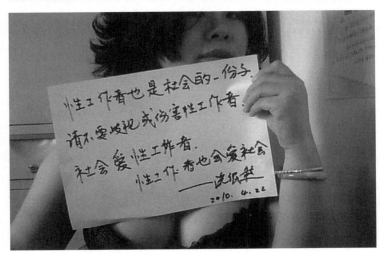

Figure 16: Sister Swallow compares her naked body to that of a model. She also holds a sign in defense of sex workers. Photocredit Jin Ge (金葛).

appealed to the legal system in an attempt to clear her name. She eventually stopped the fight and cancelled her account when people started making comments about her daughter.

Like Mu Zimei, Sister Swallow is a libertine and a proponent of "pure casual sex," as she theorizes: "Sex with total strangers is most pure, you do not need to be a hypocrite, all you need to do is coitus with all your heart and soul," Or as she states in a more poetic frame of mind:

I only hope that I can mediate Yin and Yang so that the blood can run through my veins quickly and happily, releasing all the energy. At that moment, Yin and Yang are integrated into one, and nature and human are integrated into one. Then I take a shower and go to sleep. The next day, I am fresh and I get back to my routine job. It doesn't matter who that man is. I only need the effect.

When I asked Sister Swallow how she recalls those large-scale attacks on her blog, she replies that they were overplayed in the media:

When I posted my pictures, half of the people actually supported me publicly and didn't consider it to be weird. The rest could not understand it and considered my blog to be cheap publicity ... Sadly, most of the netizens could not rationally appreciate mature women, since they so adore the beauty of youth.

When I asked her further how she strategizes as a mature woman to find lovers and friends, she answers that she tries to see the benefits of the age gap:

I think that men prefer different women and also want variety in terms of age. I have found that many young men really love mature women (especially women who are married), while old men like younger girls. I guess the former need to learn, and the latter are being nostalgic. [6]

Sister Swallow gradually became an activist and feminist fighting for the rights for sex workers. She currently maintains a website devoted to sex workers' rights and also maintains a personal blog on Sina.com

She opened the website Hongchen2006.com (紅塵網), which in the Chinese language means: "The World of Playboys and Slutty Women." It is a website free of discrimination and humiliation, condemning sexual violence and harmful actions against sex workers. It also provides a platform for gender and legal issues, sex-worker's rights, birth-control, abortion and information about HIV. As the hostess of the hotline, Sister Swallow offers advice for sex workers. She is there to help them personally, offering kind words and support for their profession:

I have experienced emotional and marital issues. I am willing to hear your story and help you solve your problem. Since I am a woman, I understand about female bodies and genitals. Please trust me and tell me your true story. I have lawyers and experts to consult when you need legal help or HIV information. In case you ask my motivation for all of this, I'll tell you now: it is because I am a woman, a mother, who has suffered and has come from a rural background.

She also writes to the male visitors:

When you face a sex worker, please don't forget that besides being a woman, she is a mother of a kid and a daughter of some mother. So please treat her nicely.

Off-line, she organizes and participates in social activities, including organizing a Sex Worker's Day, hosting a hot-line for sex workers, and establishing a Chinese Female Rights Workshop. Besides providing information on HongCheng2006.com and maintaining personal websites, she also gives practical advice on Twitter. For instance she tells sex workers that they can take a small card when walking the streets in case of police raids. The card will explain to the police that it is not illegal to stand on the streets. She strongly identifies with sex workers and divulges that she sometimes sleeps with men in order to get funding for her organization. She shares a story of having sex in a car with a man who asks her afterwards how he can help her out. She asks him to donate money to fund a video project, and then brags about her feat on Twitter (even though she did not enjoy having sex in a car).

When I asked her about government support for her work with sex workers, she replied both negatively and positively, indicating that she is not sure how to tackle this question. She explains that local governments provide some funding for her work, but she also rants about them, and generally makes fun of government bureaucracies. In one of her tweets she circulates a famous rant by Cheng Yi (程益中) chief editor of Nanfang Metropolitan Newspaper (南方都市報) and Xinjing Newspaper (新京報) who wrote:

The education department is the enemy of education, the hygiene department is the enemy of hygiene, the football association is the enemy of football, the writers' association is the enemy of writer's works, the consumers' association is the enemy of consumers, the film bureau is the enemy of films, the department of broadcasting and TV is the enemy of broadcasting and TV, the news department is the enemy of news and the truth department is the enemy of truth.

This rant was further and massively circulated by several Chinese people who enjoyed its poetic and cynical outlook. At this point, online activism is Sister Swallow's first and foremost goal, as she wants to use networks in order to disseminate information and provide updates about her grassroots activities. She sees herself as a feminist but does not believe in feminist theory, as she believes in doing things rather than theorizing them. She complains about mainstream academics because they only care about "high-class problems," such as a defense of homosexuality or non-monogamous relationships. However, she does express her appreciation of academic figures like Dr. Li Yinhe and Pan Suiming (潘綏銘) though she remains skeptical about the role of academia in helping along sex culture:

> Academics love to do research and read. However, actually almost all erotic activities would come from the grassroots levels. Academics have never wanted anything to happen, they are just doing their research after the real things have already happened. I think an academic expert who specializes in sex/sexuality may have very little sex, maybe he/she cannot perform it even once in a month.

In short, Sister Swallow is critical of the academic profession in helping sex-work activism. She sees herself as a different breed and manages to turn her moment of instant fame into a productive long-term social and activist career. Rather than totally succumbing to the ecstasies of love, she reinvents herself over and over again as a blogger, eventually becoming China's leading sexpert.

Conclusion

It is shown that the legacy of activist bloggers is different from that of sex bloggers, but these two forces do complement each other in a quest for unadulterated entertainment and public sex culture. The 2010 White Paper on Chinese Internet Policy announced that China has 220 million bloggers and that a large percentage of netizens take part in public debates. Despite the bragging tone of the White Paper, we know from different sources that all blogging content is controlled and actively censored and that many at the core of dissident blogging are sometimes harassed and detained by the government. Nonetheless the Chinese Internet has spawned a generation of "fierce bloggers" who are willing to take up sensitive topics and, among other things, criticize the Chinese government's war on pornography. The political blogging culture fights back against the "propaganda of impotence," producing witty commentaries about the necessity of sexual entertainment and the positive examples of porn stars. As a matter of fact, one of the most well-liked Japanese porn stars, Sola Aoi, received the title of "People's Artist with both Virtues and Professional Skills" as she demonstrated her love for Chinese culture through various comments and actions on the Twitter network.

Besides the contributions of gonzo journalism, the Chinese blogosphere is humorous and ephemeral, a bit like the western 1960s' nudist performance pieces or the act of streaking in public spaces. Bloggers make bold statements against conservative morality and have to deal with hostility from the agents of surveillance and censorship. According to Farrer (2007), it is exactly a dialogic consciousness that constitutes a threat to the centralized Communist authority. In almost all cases, these contributions of bloggers show a new kind of sexual pride and individualism, but they are equally subject to harassment and ridicule by conservative-leaning mobs. Bloggers find creative ways to appear and disappear on the Internet while building strengths to keep defending eroticism, sex play and libertinism.

Notes

1. At the time of the much bigger and more devastating Japanese earthquake and tsunami in March 2011, I could not find any evidence of Sola Aoi initiating a fundraise campaign. Her Twitter account went dead for a couple of weeks and she resurfaced when traveling to Indonesia to promote her role in a new non-pornographic horror movie, Evil Nurse 2.
2. As for the sex diary of Han Feng, the original thread disappeared but was re-uploaded on Tianya. cn http://www.tianya.cn/publicforum/content/free/1/1822352.shtml as 'Full text of Han Feng bureau chief and his lover Tan Shanfang's sex diary' (accessed 15 July 2011).
3. The blogger LoveAi - LoveAiWeiWei analysis of the 50 Cents Army can be found at http://loveaiww. blogspot.com/2011/04/blog-post_3788.html (accessed 12 July 2011).
4. The Li Xiaoguai Cartoon "Recycle Bin" can be found at http://blogtd.org/2009/02/27/recycle-bin/ (accessed 12 July 2011).
5. My interview with Dr. Li Yinhe, Chinese Academy of Social Sciences took place in Beijing, 20 March, 2010.
6. My interview with Sister Swallow was carried out online and took place in November-December 2009.

References

Agence France-Press (2010) "Pop Star Detained in Indonesia's first celebrity sex video scandal," *South China Morning Post,* 23 June.

Ai Wei Wei Blog Excerpt (2009) in Zhai Minglei, Zhong Guo Meng Bo and Chan Wun Ying (eds) *China's Fierce Bloggers, The Power of Civil Discourses in the Age of New Media,* Hong Kong, Tiandi Book, September, pp. 43–47. Ai Weiwei's blog is located at http://www.bullogger.com/blogs/aiww (accessed 11 July 2011).

Bandurski, David (2011) "Global Times Attacks Ai Wei Wei and the West," Posted for *China Media Project.* Available at http://cmp.hku.hk/2011/04/07/11340/ (accessed 7 May 2011).

Burns, Simon (2006) "Nude bloggers upset China beauty contest," *V3.co.uk*, 25 May, http://www.v3.co.uk/vnunet/news/2156937/china-bloggers-beauty-contest (accessed 19 July 2011).

Chien, Eugenia (2005) "China's Sexual Blogolution," posted on *Alternet.org*, 12 Nov, http://www.alternet.org/story/28145/china%27s_sexual_blogolution (accessed 13 July 2011)

CNN.com (2010) "China's Rebel Blogger," 4 June, http://edition.cnn.com/2010/TECH/web/06/03/han.han.china/index.html (accessed 8 July 2011).

Cody, Edward (2005) "In Chinese Cyberspace, a Blossoming Passion," *The Washington Post,* (online) 19 July, http://www.washingtonpost.com/wp-dyn/content/article/2005/07/18/AR2005071801561.html (accessed 19 July 2011).

Farrer, James (2007) "China's Women Sex Bloggers and Dialogic Sexual Politics on the Chinese Internet," *China Aktuell*, 36: 4, pp.9–45.

UNIVERSITY OF WINCHESTER
LIBRARY

February Girl (2006) "Exposed? Immoral? Get undressed!" 1 March, http://blog.sina.com.cn/s/blog_48c22252010002se.html This blog post was translated into English on *EastSouthWestNorth* blog http://www.zonaeuropa.com/20060312_1.htm, March 2006 (accessed 15 July 2011).

Fei, Na (2010) 我从不妄自菲薄--专访日本女优苍井空 wo cong bu wang zi fei bo – zhuan fang ri ben nv you cang jing kong (I never look down upon myself – Interview with Japanese actress Sola Aoi), *Nanfang Weekend,* (online), June 23, http://www.infzm.com/content/46724 (accessed 11 July 2011).

Han Han (2009) Blog Excerpt, in Zhai Minglei, Zhong Guo Meng Bo and Chan Wun Ying eds., *China's Fierce Bloggers, The Power of Civil Discourses in the Age of New Media*, Hong Kong, Tiandi Book, (pp. 73–99). Han Han's blog is located at http://blog.sina.com.cn/twocold (accessed 11 July 2011).

Ho, Josephine (2010) "Censorship and Sensibility," Keynote lecture at *International Communication Association* Conference, Singapore, 26 June.

Jacobs, Andrew (2010) "Heartthrob's Blog Challenges China's Leaders," *New York Times* (online) 12 March, http://www.nytimes.com/2010/03/13/world/asia/13Han Han.html (accessed 11 July 2011).

Jiang, Liuqiao (2010) 安徽一贪官被曝与500女性有染 妻子发现 "性爱日记" an hui yi tan guan bei bao yu 500 nv xing you ran, qi zi fa xian xing ai ri ji. (A corrupted officer was caught having affairs with 500 women. The wife found the "Sex Diary") *Anhuinews.com* (online) 7 April, http://politics.people.com.cn/GB/14562/11307497.html (accessed 11 July 2011).

Jones, Gary (2007) "The Blogger Who Took on China," 12 February, http://www.thefirstpost.co.uk/2231,news-comment,news-politics,the-blogger-who-took-on-china (accessed 11 July 2011).

Li, Hao (2011) "College Girls Promotes Nude Art," *Shenzhen Daily*, (online) 4 March, http://www.szdaily.com/content/2011-03/04/content_5396842.htm (accessed 11 July 2011).

Lian, Yue (2009) Blog Excerpt, "Cross the River By Feeling Nipples," in Zhai Minglei, Zhong Guo Meng Bo and Chan Wun Ying (eds) *China's Fierce Bloggers, The Power of Civil Discourses in the Age of New Media* . Hong Kong, Tiandi Book (p. 41). Lian Yue's blog can be found at www.lianyue.net (第八大洲 the eighth continent) (accessed 16 July 2011).

Luo, Yanghuo (2009) Blog Excerpt, in Zhai Minglei, Zhong Guo Meng Bo and Chan Wun Ying (eds.) *China's Fierce Bloggers, The Power of Civil Discourses in the Age of New Media*, Hong Kong, Tiandi Book (pp. 232–38).

Lam, Oi-Wan and Ip, Iam-Chong (eds) (2009) *Info Rhizome: report on independent media in the Chinese-speaking world*, Hong Kong: Hong Kong In-Media.

Lyon, David (2007) *Surveillance Studies: An Overview,* Malden MA: Polity Press.

McBeth, John (2010) "Moral Outrage Smacks of Hypocrisy," *The Straits Times*, 26 June.

Merewether, Charles (2008) "Ruins in Reverse," *Ai Weiwei: Under Construction* (catalogue), Sydney: NSW Press.

Nip, Amy (2010) "Censors delete 95pc of Blogs a Day, Forum Told," *South China Morning Post*, 20 June.

Quartly, James (2010) "Believe in Sister Phoenix. It only took 100 years," *China Daily* (online) 10 March, http://www.chinadaily.com.cn/life/2010-03/10/content_9566092.htm (accessed 11 July 2011).

Rofel, Lisa (2007) *Desiring China: Experiments in Neoliberalism, Sexuality, and Public Culture*, Durham: Duke University Press.

Schokora, Adam J. (2009) "Ai Wei Wei Naked," *56 Minus One Blog, 2* June, http://56minus1.com/2009/05/ai-weiwei-naked (accessed 11 July 2011).

Schokora, Adam J. (2008) " China's first blogger on the Chinese blogosphere," Danwei.org, 6 August, http://www.danwei.org/Internet/isaac_mao_and_the_chinese_blog.php (accessed 11 July 2011).

Shi, Jingtao (2011) "Ai Wei Wei Accused of Huge Tax Scam," *South China Morning Post*, 21 May.

Skirmisher (2007) "Living in a Glass House: China's Version," Posted on *Skirmisher*.org, 16 May, http://skirmisher.org/culture/living-in-a-glass-house-chinas-version (accessed 8 July 2011).

The Telegraph (2008) "Chinabounder Sex Blogger Reveals His Identity", *Telegraph.co.uk* (online) 17 July, http://www.telegraph.co.uk/news/worldnews/asia/china/2420969/ChinaBounder-sex-blogger-reveals-his-identity.html (accessed July 8 2011).

Tiger Temple (2009) Blog Excerpt, in Zhai Minglei, Zhong Guo Meng Bo and Chan Wun Ying eds, *China's Fierce Bloggers, The Power of Civil Discourses in the Age of New Media*. Hong Kong, Tiandi Book (pp. 147–71). Tiger Temple's blogs can be found on the following site http://24hour.blogbus.com (accessed 19 June 2010).

Wilde, Jonathan (2005) "The Emancipation of Mumu," *Distributed Republic Blog*, (online) 30 November, http://www.distributedrepublic.net/archives/2005/11/30/the-emancipation-of-mu-mu (accessed 11 July 2011).

Xiao, Qang (2010) "Han Han Person of the Year and his New Magazine," *China Digital Times* (online) 10 January, http://chinadigitaltimes.net/2010/01/han-han-%E9%9F%A9%E5%AF%92-person-of-the-year-2009-and-his-new-magazine/ (accessed 15 July 2011).

Xinhua Agency (2010) "China Issues White Paper on Internet Policy," 8 June, http://china.org.cn/china/2010-06/08/content_20206978_3.htm (accessed 11 July 2011).

Zhai, Minglei, Zhong Guo Meng Bo and Chan Wun Ying (eds), *China's Fierce Bloggers, The Power of Civil Discourses in the Age of New Media*. Tiandi Book, Hong Kong, September 2009.

Zhai, Minglei (2009) Blog Excerpt, in Zhai Minglei, Zhong Guo Meng Bo and Chan Wun Ying (eds), *China's Fierce Bloggers, The Power of Civil Discourses in the Age of New Media* (pp 483), Hong Kong: Tiandi Book. Zhang Minglei's blogs are located at www.1bao.org, http://www.bulloger.com/blogs/1bao (accessed 16 June 2010).

Chapter 3

Gender Variations on the Aching Sex Scene: Young Adult Fe/Male Responses to Explicit Media and Internet Culture

Introduction: The Fe/Male Romance with Internet Porn Culture

The third chapter continues a search for enlightened porn culture in China and Hong Kong, where sexually explicit materials are circulating on the Internet or in semi-legal retail outlets. The chapter looks at the different ways in which women and men express arousal in response to sexually explicit materials. Since women have not cultivated seasoned viewing habits, their stated desires for soft-core products and sex talk opens up a fuzzy space for pleasure and awareness. Wendy Chun (2006) points out in *Control and Freedom: Power and Paranoia and the Age of Cyber Optics* that a web user's tendency to create sexual diaries and archives is part of a will to knowledge. In *The History of Sexuality*, vol 1 *The Will To Knowledge*, Foucault (1990) explains the functioning of sexuality as an analysis of power related to the emergence of a science of sexuality ("scientia sexualis"). He criticizes the repressive hypothesis, or the widespread belief that we have repressed our natural sexual drives. He shows that what we think of as repression of sexuality actually constitutes sexuality as a core feature of our identities, and has produced a proliferation of sex and pornography discourses. This force not only lies in the search for sexual arousal or relationships, or the testing of moral boundaries and social norms, but also in the urge to build a new knowledge apparatus around habits of navigating and manipulating the products of sex culture itself.

In *One for the Girls: The Pleasures and practices of Reading Women's Porn*, Clarissa Smith discusses UK women's reactions to pornography through an in-depth analysis of a women's porn magazine and through in-depth interviews with readers. Smith criticizes both feminist and religion-driven anti-pornography scholars who make pessimistic generalizations and consistently refuse to research specific porn and erotica cultures. For instance, the most frequently cited US anti-pornography feminist, Andrea Dworkin, attacks pornography from an essentialist position of anger that "ignores a whole range of differences – not least media forms, textual structures and narrative strategies in favor of a focus on male power." Smith wants to revisit Dworkin's central claim that the male viewer understands pornography via his identification and approval of its power to render women as objects (Smith 2007: 36).

Smith's focus on female porn users makes an intervention in Dworkin's unproven lineage of male physical violence. Smith also criticizes older psychoanalytic readings of pornography that are overly focused on an imagined phallic male subject. In either case, these traditions have ignored soliciting testimonies from women who indeed also get turned on by identifying with stories of sex and power. She believes that female porn users have indeed contributed to a productive kind of social upheaval. Theoretically speaking, Smith relies on newer psychoanalytical studies by Laura Kipnis, who believes that the plain, vulgar and unromanticized bodies of pornography construct a space of female awakening by targeting the powerfully-integrated emotions of lust and disgust (Kipnis 1996: 94). The grunting and sweating bodies of porn accompany women's desire to experience "low" culture and some of its socially unacceptable mindsets. The most vulgar bodies of porn are indeed typically outlawed in most public venues of art and culture, but can provide a social service by unleashing a contradictory awareness of desire and inhibition, a powerful feeling of stimulation involving a loss of control (Smith 2007: 43).

My study investigates this awareness through interviews with women and men from Hong Kong and mainland China in 2008–2009. Through in-depth interviews with sixty university students aged 18–25, and an anonymous fixed-response survey carried out on the Internet between July 2007 and May 2009, cultural reactions to "base culture" were elicited and analyzed. Chinese young adults are fostering attitudes of social unrest around base culture. Our strategy was to dig into self-articulations of sexual pleasure and knowledge in relation to its specific media texts.

A second aim is to question Chinese cultural myths of abstinence that deny or stigmatize these testimonies of individual sexual awakening. One of these myths concerns female frigidity, in which women's lack of arousal is seen as a normal state of being, or a strategic and well-conceived position of submission within the patriarchal culture and its phallocentric sexuality (Pei et al. 2007: 08). The chapter shows that Chinese women's ambivalence about sexually explicit materials does not stem from frigidity and submission, but from a positive desire for social change and alternative depictions of power and gender in acts of love.

These positive voices demanding sexual stimulation and social change have become active in the era of digital networks. The growth of online social networks for friendship and sexuality has caused rebellion against traditional patriarchal parameters in countries around the world. New Internet laws and methods of surveillance have been put into place that try to temper the sexual worldviews of young adults who find themselves readily involved in the "vulgar" tangents of Internet culture. Many of the attempts at heightened censorship in China, Hong Kong, and in countries around the globe, stem from ad hoc proposals from conservative religious groups and politicians whose knowledge of culture rarely matches that of Internet youth and young adults.

Moreover, in many leading debates and policy documents, pornography is often poorly and narrowly defined as commercial hard-core movies. Women's potential positive identification with varying types of sexually explicit media and their desires for diversified media texts are rarely brought to the table in discussions of how to formulate policy. In other words, gender difference or women's lack of arousal is a convenient excuse for either banning or repackaging pornography as highly-commercial "male-stream" culture. But there are indeed more holistic views on sexually explicit media that encompass a wider range of concepts of power and gender. Following the views of Clarissa Smith and Laura

Kipnis, the chapter tries to locate a positive outcome in the Chinese women's identification with sexually explicit materials.

Our intention to gather information from Internet consumers about this sensitive topic turned out to be a very difficult. We started out with a general effort to locate dispersed interviewees and informants who were willing to talk but, at a later stage, we became more focused on student groups and their self-articulations of sexual pleasure and gender difference. The research activities were partially supported by a Strategic Research Grant funded from City University of Hong Kong (香港城市大學), entitled "Internet Pornography, Global Networks & Cyber Identities in Hong Kong" (香港的網絡色情、全球社交網絡與網絡身份), which was an interdisciplinary inquiry and collaboration between the liberal arts and social sciences that sought to elicit and investigate responses to the widening cultures and changing economies of Internet pornography.

Internet pornography is defined as people's use of new digital technologies and the networks for the production and distribution of sexually explicit materials (Jacobs 2007). They include legal and illegal sites for commercial products, home-made materials, personal blogs, story-telling sites and artistic galleries.

As I have shown in Chapter 1, young Chinese men are mostly hooked on Japanese Adult Videos. Many of them favor the look of Asian body types and youthful porn stars who embody innocence and submission, which allows them a masculine sense of conquest. Western models and porn stars are considered too coarse or too sexually forward and do not suit their specific tastes and desires. While many women officially accept these male fantasies, they also express coldness and frustration towards them. Additionally, many women admit to feeling excluded from debates about sexually explicit media and feeling trapped in an atmosphere of social taboo. They would like to watch and discuss sex culture but they find that Chinese culture has opened up little space for their participation. As stated by Tabby:

> In Europe one can discuss sexual topics. Here in Hong Kong, females still have to learn how to express their fantasies and inner selves in order to have a more balanced view about pornography. Simply, females should be more dominant and they should find out how to be emotionally and physically satisfied.

The study thus sets out to address this recurring note of frustration without being solely focused on female notions of enjoyment and alienation.

Notes on Interviewing Methods

We posted a survey in both English and Chinese between April and October 2008. The survey links were posted on the project website and were further distributed on online forums such as Discuss.com and University bbs. We received answers from about 321 residents. In the English version of the survey, we received about 70 per cent female answers versus 30 per cent male answers, while the Chinese version had more or less equal female and male respondents.

About 70 per cent of the respondents belong to the age group of 18–29 and had most likely been recruited by university students. The ethnicity of respondents in the Chinese version is predominantly Hong Kong Chinese, while 30 per cent of respondents in the English version belong to various non-Chinese ethnicities. Even though, to a certain degree, most respondents are consumers of sexually explicit media, very few are actually willing to pay money for their transactions. They are used to downloading the materials for free and further share them with actual friends or anonymous netfriends. Since our respondent groups are somewhat female-dominated, it is interesting to see that women have indeed become involved in the downloading and sharing of sexually explicit media.

As for interviewing rounds, we carried out in-depth conversations with about fifteen web users who were willing to be interviewed in front of their computers while explaining their feelings and ideas about specific images and web sites. Additionally, we interviewed local academic experts and activists such Lam Oiwan (林藹雲) and Verdy Leung (梁偉儀), who helped contextualize current debates about Internet pornography in Chinese culture. Finally, in Fall 2008 and Spring 2009, we conducted 45-minute interviews with about sixty university students from Hong Kong and mainland China. These interviews were carried out with a team of student assistants to help create a comfortable environment for dialogues amongst peers. The interviews were based on a set of questions which we shared amongst interviewers but which we did not follow in any systematic order. Rather, we took an open approach in soliciting information and followed the personal cues of the participants themselves. The participants were selected on a voluntary basis from several large university classes. These students had been very active in in-class discussions, and they were happy to reflect on their feelings and to exchange more personal information. They also contacted their fellow students and friends and encouraged them to participate in the study.

The interviews were carried out in the English language, which allowed students to express the values of an "educated self" and rely on concepts that we had discussed in classrooms. Since English is the primary language of instruction at City University of Hong Kong, student mostly felt competent enough to express themselves, even though it is not their native language. The students were very honest and open in these interviews, even though, it should be admitted, they may have provided different views and emotions if we had interviewed students in their native languages, Cantonese or Mandarin.

A large percentage of interviewees are university students From Hong Kong and China in the 18–25 age group who were taking courses in the department of Media and Communication at City University of Hong Kong. Almost all male interviewees report downloading sexually explicit media through non-commercial channels of distribution such as Internet-based forums, web blogs and chat rooms. They use the Internet to download and share products, which are different from the selections that they can find in DVD/VCD retail outlets. Women navigate into sexually explicit content in a typically less focused manner and "stumble onto" a variety of samples that have become part of their daily online usage. Some of them use sexually explicit media for sexual arousal, but others just glance at it and quickly move onto other things. Nonetheless, these furtive glances seem to have indeed left an imprint on them. Even if women are less knowledgeable about sexually explicit materials and less eager to consume them, they also show a higher degree of involvement in the research project.

Cultural Cataclysm: The Edison Chen Sex Scandal

February 2008 became an opportune moment to interview people as DIY pornography had become the subject of a widely-reported news item. China and Hong Kong experienced a six-week-long national media scandal around the DIY pornography collection of celebrity entertainer, Edison Chen (陳冠希), dubbed the "Nude Photos Incident" (淫照事件) or "Sex Photos Gate" (艷照門).[1] Chen's self-created photos of his private sex sessions with other Chinese celebrities had been leaked onto the Internet without his permission. These privately-made pictures revealed a degree of intimacy and explicitness that staggered audiences, though they would be less shocking to anyone familiar with online porn culture. The scandal triggered an enormous amount of heated discussion in the mass media and classrooms. Since most of our students were intensely affected by this media event, we took some time to analyze their feelings and reactions.

We found out that nearly all the student interviewees and survey participants had looked at this collection of photos. The mass media and entertainment companies tried to maintain a

Figure 1: Views from the Nude Photo Gate Incident. While tabloid media presented Chen as a bully who had managed to seduce the starlets of "innocence" – Bobo Chan and Gillian Chung – the photos themselves show a different picture as the starlets look happy and proud to be involved. Digital drawings by Bonni Rambatan.

conservative-patriarchal view by showing that the female celebrities had been manipulated by Edison Chen. Chen was forced to issue two televised apologies and one of the female lovers, Gillian Chung (鍾欣桐), appeared twice to make her own tearful confession and to act out the role of victim. Most interviewees had looked at these TV appearances and believed that these female confessions were dishonest, that the women involved had actually consented to have sex with Edison Chen and to partake voluntarily in the photography sessions. We asked our interviewees if they thought of these women as victims, and they replied:

(F1) No, I do not think that they are victims because they had a love affair with Edison Chen and they were willing to take the pictures together and they also showed sexy poses or smilingly showed off their sexy lingerie.

(F2) I do not really think they are really victims, because they knew that they were taking pictures with Edison Chen. They knew that they were being video recorded, so they knew the consequences after that.

We also asked students about the cultural impact of the scandal on people's values and experiences with Internet pornography. For some female students, the incident indicated that Chinese society was unforgiving towards sexually-open women while "the guys can get away with it."

(F1) I think that the guys always have had the freedom to make love to different girls. In Chinese society in the past, the husband could feel free to end the relationship but the wife could not, so I think it is the guys who will always have more power.

(F2) It is hard for women to show their interest in sex, because they will be thought of as bad women, because a good woman in Chinese culture should be very submissive, and they definitely should not talk about sex that in an active way, or initiate a conversation like that.

For many students, the incident had a positive effect on social values, as it opened up friends and families to discuss these new trends in sexuality. Even though they were not used to discussing sex within the family, the scandal unleashed emotive responses of tolerance and shock within the family. Some interviewees saw this as a moment of transformation or liberation, as indicated by one male student:

(M1) I think that society will be more open because, before this incident, HK people were quite conservative about sex. In my family for instance, before Edison Chen, we seldom discussed sex issues because my mother is quite conservative in some cases. But after the incident we found that we could discuss sex more often than before. Yes, it helped my family talk about sex and pornography.

Fe/Male Notions of Intimacy and Arousal

As had become clear in responses to the scandal, Chinese young adults are cultivating positive and refined reactions to sexually explicit media, which goes in tandem with their maturing Internet-based agencies. But how do men and women differ in their overall reactions to sexually explicit media? In trying to get answers to this question, young men reply that they are simply satisfied with the wide availability of pornographic products while women often indicate that they feel alienated from them. Women are happy to participate in our interviews but their statements often drift into a disclosure of personal desires and love affairs. For instance, Sum shares an intimate and funny story about her first Internet date:

> In the past few years when ICQ was popular, I tried to use ICQ to meet new friends. They were really anonymous friends but I decided to meet up with somebody at a bus stop. It was funny, because at that time I did not know what to do, and I thought that it would be ok to bring him home. I brought him up to my home that day. And my mum and brother and father were not there. But once I took a good look at him, I felt I didn't want to let him into my home, because he was not that handsome anyway. But still I took him inside as I thought we were still on a date and I wanted to be friendly. I brought him home and we did nothing, we just sat down and chatted. And suddenly my mum was back, and I was in a panic, so I buried him in my wardrobe so that there seemed to be nothing going on. And once my mum and my brother came in, my brother asked "Why is there another pair of shoes here?" And then I said they were my father's. And he said, "No, our father does not have these kinds of shoes," and I felt embarrassed. So I opened my wardrobe and let my friend come out, and let my mum see him. I told my mum, sorry my friend just came here and he's going now, and then I brought him back to the bus stop and let him go, and that is the first time I met a male friend through the Internet.

Sum was the active or inquisitive party within this date, in seducing a man and picking him up from the bus stop and delivering him back at the same spot several hours later. Even though her family controlled her decisions, she was able to thoroughly check out potential lovers. The ability for young people to date and mate through new communication technologies has created a sexual mutiny of kinds, and has revitalized dating practices at a much younger age. Young adults pursue affairs that are less habituated by parental control. As confirmed by a male interviewee, Yang Shuo:

> For example, in our parents' time, if they wanted to be in a relationship or they wanted to start dating early, they could only write letters to each other. They didn't even have phones. They could only date somewhere and then set another time for the next date. But in our times, we have our phones at home so we can easily make phone calls. And for the post-90s generation, they can do it through peer-to-peer communication, from one person directly to another person, for instance by using the mobile phone. For instance, if I want to call a

girl at home, she may not be the one who picks up the phone. Maybe her parents would pick up and ask me "Why are you looking for her?" and then I would quickly hang up the phone. But now, I can contact her directly. Then the relationship can start earlier.

Yang's wish to "start earlier" is consistent with his desire to develop a good love life and to be in favor of sexually explicit materials, as he later states in the interview. Through the new access to Internet culture and its social expectations, youngsters can more freely contact each other and forward materials about sex and romance as a peer-to-peer type of education. In this vein of connectedness, almost all of our interviewees testify that they forwarded Edison Chen's sex images, while some explain that these acts of sharing were a way of trying out social contacts. We also found out that males are more used to these peer-to-peer channels, while women are less exposed to it and would maintain a less intense type of contact.

But rather than seeing women's tentative immersion as a lack of sexual interest, it can be simply thought of as a different entry into a knowledge of sex culture. In 2006 a pioneering study examined Chinese women and their sexual gaze and found that they have indeed become agents, speakers and creators of sexual worlds. Ho and Tsang carefully tracked women's self-articulations of a sexualized gaze, more specifically their knowledge of the penis, as an exploration of the self and sexual growth. They set out to investigate the relationship between regulatory practices of such knowledge and secret "ruptures," which were seen as powerful sources of excitement and bonding. Through these ruptures women were able "to break the rules and experience the forbidden which has always been a source of excitement and fascination" (Ho and Tsang 2002: 65).

It was found that young women were, overall, rather alert and eager to break away from the predictable role of the silent or subdued sexual being. This misconception is still prevalent in Hong Kong's discourses concerning the female sex, due to a coalescence of Chinese conservative morality, the political power of Christian groups, and patriarchal social habits in capitalist workplaces. Women increasingly want to find release from these labels and other normalized expectations at home and work.

American and Canadian sexologists working as clinical psychologists have been equally interested in gendered patterns of excitement in response to sexually explicit media. Their methods of measuring reactions and arousal are very different from those used by cultural theorists. They try to measure psychophysiological responses to sexually explicit media, rather than relying on interviews and self-reported testimonies. In "Selecting Films for Sex Research: Gender difference in Erotic Film Preference," a 2003 study carried out in the Kinsey institute, researchers first set out to measure whether or not women would be less "biologically wired" than men to respond to pornography (Janssen 2003). Since previous studies of arousal had been male-dominated in content selections, female researchers were asked to compile a wider variety of "female-friendly" sexually explicit content. It was found that women responded more positively to these female-friendly selections in comparison to the more "typically male" film clips. But even though women responded positively, they did not report arousal levels comparable to those of men.

A more in-depth breakthrough concerning female arousal was made in 2004 by Meredith Chivers, whose study "A Sex Difference in the Specificity of Sexual Arousal," found that heterosexual women and lesbians respond positively to a wide range of straight and queer sexual pairings. In this study, male genital arousal was assessed with penile plethysmography, using a mercury-in-rubber strain gauge to measure changes in the circumference of the penis as erection developed. Female and male-to-female transsexual genital arousal was assessed via a change in vaginal pulse amplitude (VPA) with a vaginal photoplethysmograph. In addition, subjective arousal or lack of arousal was assessed continuously through self-reporting by using a lever moving through a 180-degree arc.

According to the outcomes of these new tests, women would be equally "biologically wired" to like sexually explicit media, but they would have different patterns of arousal. They identify more easily with varying sexual preferences, while heterosexual and homosexual men are less flexible and tend to favor one specific type of sexual preference. Female arousal thus became characterized as more open-ended than male sexuality, with greater intra-individual variation in preferences, behaviors, attitudes, and responsiveness to cultural influences (Chivers 2004). Chivers was inconclusive about whether or not these gender differences were innate or culturally influenced but seemed to favor the former explanation. Her work became widely popularized in the USA and her results were taken up by other scholars who argued against the categorization of female arousal as inborn or innate.

Women's open-ended responses can be caused by a variety of factors, including a lack of established feminine porn culture or the need to be immersed as part of social change. But even if female-oriented sites and products are still sparse in Chinese culture, women do have easy access to them through global media networks. An example would be the website www. crashpadseries.com, which grew out of the expanding fanbase of Shine Louise Houston's lesbian cult porn movie *The Crashpad* (2005). The site became a social network and member site for women to upload DIY sex images and make contact with other like-minded women. Women internationally have been drawn to this site as it promotes images of dyke-like bodies and transgendered sexuality often marginalized in their local cultures. Other examples of product-specific sexual desires were examined by Clarissa Smith in her in-depth study of British female readers of the soft-core magazine *For Women* (Smith 2007). Her aim was to survey responses to this peculiar UK magazine while tracking the circulation of cultural debates and attitudes about pornography. Smith's study reveals that British women have mixed emotions about the male nude models, but their confident and lengthy testimonies also show a type of social refinement about pornography that was unprecedented in the UK.

The question we attempt to address is how Chinese women and men experience sexual excitement as part of cultural life-styles and modes of social change. We did not follow reactions to one peculiar media text but about a wider range of movies and media, including the images of the Edison Chen sex scandal and Ang Lee's movie *Lust, Caution*. Chivers' findings on the open-endedness of female arousal are socially progressive, but they do not take into account the cultural flows of sex as social expectations. By interviewing university students about their social habits and ideological views, we tried to find if and out how the new generations of Internet browsers make efforts to transgress social conventions.

Fe/Male Sexual Subjectivities

Table 1: Profiles of Male Research Participants

Name	Culture/Religion/Educational Background	Self-Description of Netporn Tastes and Habits
Leo	Mainland China Buddhist 4th year undergraduate	Internet downloader via forums, shares via MSN or ICQ or QQ. Watches a few times per month. Shares with male friends only. Porn is not good for his girlfriend, but he did send her the Edison Chen photos. Prefers Japanese over Western, less "fake." Does not like lesbian porn because of use of dildos instead of the "real" thing. Believes DIY porn will be a growing trend.
Lee	Hong Kong Catholic 3rd year undergraduate	Downloads and shares since high school (with 56k modem); now downloads via HK Discuss forum, watches twice a week. Shares with male friends. Watched with girlfriend once but there was "just a little spark." Enjoys Japanese and Western alike. Disgusted by lesbian porn, maybe because of his religion. Worried about his little brother who is into feminine cartoons like "Sailor Moon."
AMJ	Mainland China No religion 3rd year undergraduate	Downloads from forums. Often shares and discusses with male friends; but only "shallow" sharing with females – as a little joke. Prefers commercial porn over DIY but believes DIY will be a growing trend. Prefers Japanese over Western because Western girls are "too active" "too enthusiastic" while Japanese girls pretend to "resist"; does not like local HK products either because of Cantonese language. Does not believe Mainland is more or less open abour sex/porn than HK, just individual differences.

Name	Culture/Religion/Educational Background	Self-Description of Netporn Tastes and Habits
Lambert	HK No Religion 3rd year undergraduate	Does not like porn as he is traditional and his family is very strict. Sex talk in high school but not at university, feels left out. Believes Internet should be more heavily regulated as DIY web culture is out of control. Believes sex videos should be discussed in class, otherwise meaningless to youngsters.
Anthony	HK No Religion 2nd year undergraduate	Free downloading and will never pay for it. Watches 5 times a week. Prefers American over Japanese. Porn is private and he does not want to share. Does not believe he can learn anything from porn.
Elvis	HK No religion 2nd year undergraduate	Downloads via BT. Shares VCDs/DVDs with friends. Borrows from father. Has no girl friend but would like to share with her, if she agrees. Prefers Japanese over Western because of Asian body look + because Western girls are too open. Enjoys the pretense of love in porn. Not interested in DIY because he hates to witness private scenes. Was shocked by Edison Chen, esp. the images of Cecilia Cheung because she was too extreme, too enthusiastic or "open".
Maki	Korea No religion 3rd year undergraduate	Watches DIY porn as it is very popular in Korea. Most movies made with cell phones. Other forms of porn are banned. Saw the photos of Edison Chen but did not enjoy those girls – did not know female celebs and thought they were too skinny.
Josh	HK No religion 2nd year undergraduate	Tried once to watch together with girl friend but she declined. Used to watch with friend on pay-TV channels, through membership of his father. Lately friends forward links for him to download. Would be interested in making a DIY movie one day but would not upload it.

Name	Culture/Religion/Educational Background	Self-Description of Netporn Tastes and Habits
Lam	HK No religion 2nd year undergraduate	Downloads via forums and Foxy. Does not share with friends because they already have an overload of materials. Does not share with females as they are not likely to have a reaction. Has seen some DIY porn. Prefers mainland over DIY from Hong Kong. Prefers Japanese over Western because the girls are less hard-core and more passive.
Jeff	HK Religious upbringing 2nd Year undergraduate	Downloads. Prefers Japanese as it is very different from Western, because the strong male is out to conquer female. Japanese girls are more polite while Western girls are more excited. Enjoys DIY from time to time, such as students having sex. It is acceptable to him but would never upload himself.

Table 2: Profiles of Female Research Participants

Name	Culture/Religion/Educational Background	Self-Description of Netporn Tastes and habits
Alice	HK Religious upbringing 3rd year undergraduate	Prefers watching movies with sex scenes rather than "porn." Likes French movies and sex scenes which leave room for imagination. She does not like porn because of its lack of story-line. Saw Edison Chen Pictures and thinks they were nice. Chen is more like an "outsider" to HK culture while the girls were "real local HK" (more conservative – closed). DIY porn is OK. It is people's own business to do that – she does not want to watch it, though. Believes girls watch porn just to please their boyfriends.

Name	Culture/Religion/Educational Background	Self-Description of Netporn Tastes and habits
Bunny	Mainland China No Religion 3rd year undergraduate	Watched porn with her room-mate for the first time, both were shocked seeing private parts. Boyfriend in mainland sent her Edison Chen pictures via MSN, one by one. Sometimes finds porn on boyfriend's computer. They sometimes watch it together but she is not really into it. Prefers Japanese porn as it is less extreme. She prefers to watch erotic Hentai cartoons rather than "real people," but boyfriend does not like that.
Julie	Mainland China minority group No religion 3rd year undergraduate	Believes HK and mainland are both traditional and Confucian and that DIY should be considered abnormal. Edison Chen photos were her first contact with pornography. She was disgusted but nevertheless found some photos attractive. Watched porn movie with boyfriend but got bored. Believes that porn needs to have more romance. She feels neutral about people making DIY porn, but does not like how they try to be celebs. Believes that Internet should not be censored.
Sam	Hong Kong Devout Christian 3rd year undergraduate	Both her parents and her church discourage discussions about pornography. Parents used to change TV channels when sexy images come up. Believes that people should have the freedom to watch and make pornography. It would not be against her religion to join in. She is quite curious about it. Interested in Hong Kong and Japanese porn. Can sometimes enjoy erotic animations. Believes Internet is the best medium for pornography, as opposed to other venues.
Lizzy	Hong Kong Christian upbringing 3rd year undergraduate	Looked at some Edison Chen photos, but then deleted them. Feelings of guilt and prohibition. Has not seen genitals yet. Does not believe movies should have sex scenes, though she follows many arguments about that.

Name	Culture/Religion/Educational Background	Self-Description of Netporn Tastes and habits
Lesley	Hong Kong Christian upbringing 3rd year undergraduate	Only downloads and watches porn movies by accident, just watches a few minutes of it. It is not satisfying but a kind of "knowledge". Porn is mostly for male orgasm but Hong Kong girls are also getting interested. She sees HK as a mixed culture. Mixed feelings about censorship – contradictory statements. A real fan of cartoons but more about love than sex, only if sex is part of love.
Annie	Hong Kong No religion 3rd year undergraduate	She saw the Edison Chen photos but was not surprised – it is like normal celebrity behavior. Believes people can make DIY porn. It is their business. She would not as she believes she is too fat. She knows about it from forums. She downloads Japanese and other porn on HK Discuss forum when she is bored. Not very satisfying. Does not like Japanese male actors, prefers Westerners. Interested in gay porn.
Mimi	Hong Kong No religion 3rd year undergraduate	Interested in movies and TV series about sexuality. Has a lot of knowledge about this. She will only watch porn scenes if they are about relationships and if they have a message. Likes *Lust, Caution* and how they treated sex scenes. Wants to watch sexy movies with boyfriend but not porn. Used to work in DVD store and saw a lot of AV movies on shelves, lots of men were buying them along with some women too.
Miki	Hong Kong No religion 3rd year undergraduate	She does not have access to porn at home, lives in a traditional village. Saw Edison photos in class, does not believe that the women were his victims but were having fun and recording for their own memories. Believes that Internet should be free and porn should not be banned. People should be free to make DIY. It is their own business. No right or wrong about it. Her boyfriend knows a lot about this topic but they do not watch together.

Name	Culture/Religion/Educational Background	Self-Description of Netporn Tastes and habits
Cristie	Hong Kong Not religious 3rd year undergraduate	Was not at all shocked with Edison Chen photos. Believes that taking DIY photos is normal. Believes that HK people are too sensitive about sex issues.

Just Sex and Sex and Sex and Nothing Else

Women do not actively look for products but they furtively check out selections that friends and boy/girlfriends have forwarded to them. In a previous study about Chinese women and sexually explicit media, it was found that young women resist repressive attitudes precisely by casting these kinds of furtive glances (Ho and Ka 2002). It is in these "sneaky" or "stealthy" types of gazing that female agency can be located. Women feel too alienated from the "cheap" products of pornography to actually watch them for arousal. They see these types of pornography as a typically male phenomenon, a point of viewed expressed in the following statements:

[F1] Porn movies do not have a plot, they do not have a story and they do not have in-depth meaning so I am not really interested in watching those. If there would be a love story, I think it would be much better. I think that pornography is rather cheap. There is not really any artistic value, they just have sex and have sex and have sex and nothing else.

[F2] I am really not part of the porn market. I prefer romance movies or other kinds of movies. Maybe females do not have that kind of need. I think guys are the targeted audience for pornography.

[F3] Porn is more for boys, but sometimes for girls a little bit too. To make it more suitable for girls, maybe the story could be more interesting. It should not just be focused on sex or sexual intercourse. Girls do not care about sexual intercourse. They care about romance and a little bit about sex.

[F4] It's very interesting you know, my male friends, especially for the boys I hang out with, they always show great deal of interest in such things. And one of my friends, he is very interested, he told me, "if you ever want to see such movies, and if you ever have such needs, you can ask me, and I can show something to you." And then I said "Oh well, so far I don't have such kind of needs, and I also don't understand why boys love them so much." And my friend said something very interesting, he said "Well, it's a kind of male romance, you girls will never understand it." I think he's right, because I really don't understand it.

When we ask women what they do not like about pornography in general, most women answer that they want to see a cinematic narrative, or a holistic depiction of love and romance. They also indicate that they are more interested in watching movies as part of their love lives or social relationships. The larger frustration with hard-core depictions of sex reflects a desire to process sex as part of ongoing relationships. This view is consistent with Pei Yuxin and Ho Sik Ying's study of female masturbation in Shanghai which shows that sexual self-expression is easier for women in a relationship rather than for single women (Pei and Ho 2009: 516). About forty women were interviewed, many of whom enjoy masturbation as a way to improve the sexual intimacy within the relationship. Women also increasingly read and write about sex and masturbation as a "new knowledge about themselves, their bodies, sex womanhood, femininity, sexual relationships, and marriage" (Pei 2009: 521).

In short, rather than enjoying hard-core selections, women get aroused by narratives of love and approach sexual images as a new type of knowledge. They also consume different types of online sex products, as indicated by several women:

[F1] I actually like to read blogs about new products. I remember a blog that talked about interesting products, like a vibrator that you can connect to an IPod and then it will vibrate according to the music, and the rhythm of the music. That was it for me.

[F2] I prefer Japanese animation films. I like erotic animations because they have story lines. I want porn movies to tell a whole story, like a regular film story. It could be a

Figure 2: Still from Ang Lee's movie *Lust, Caution* (2008). The movie drew a huge fanbase in Hong Kong and Taiwan. It was censored in China because of the explicit sex scenes, but the deleted scenes were re-uploaded on the Chinese Internet.

romantic story or a police detective story, or a story about students or tennis players, or something like that.

Additionally, women mention Ang Lee's movie *Lust, Caution* (色戒) as an example of a sexually explicit movie that they enjoy more than pornography. They debate how and why the movie treats sexually explicit subject matter in a certain way and they admire the fact that the filmmaker pushes the boundaries of pornographic representation. While some women agree that the sex scenes are gratuitous and unnecessary within the plot, most women find them artistically accomplished as they clarify the motivations of the protagonists. As explained by one student:

[F1] I think that the movie *Lust, Caution* is a good combination of showing sex and telling a story. There are three different sex scenes, but only the first one came as quite a surprise. That is because it was too violent for me, so I just covered my eyes at that point. But after I searched for comments on the Internet, I realized that it was such a hip movie in HK and it was really a cultural phenomenon.

The social ramifications of DIY Porn

Sites for photography and video uploading are now increasingly used by couples and singles to share amateur materials and to establish friendships (Mowlabocus 2010: 73). This type of social networking is not restricted to particular genders or sexual orientations though many of the sites are, in actuality, "male domains" where a majority of male consumers determine the nature of the sexual depiction and the popularity of certain scenes. From our interviews it became clear that women have not found ways to frequently download or share DIY porn movies. Men download them in abundance and share them with each other and with their netfriends, while only tentatively sharing these materials with their girlfriends. Hence, Chinese men, both gay and straight, are ahead of the curve as consumers of internet-based DIY pornography, as indicated through different anecdotes:

(M1) I have been sharing materials with my mates since high-school but now with the Internet and the technologies of file-sharing, it is more about speed than friendship. I use Foxy and I just look at what videos are popular and going very fast. I am trying to download them as quickly as I can and use the fastest possible video player, which currently is Real player.

(M2) It is still mostly Japanese videos that I find online and trade with others. I personally like girls in costumes, like a train conductor who gets carried away by a bunch of salarymen. That one is perfect for Hong Kong. I think in a way that Chinese porn culture has been destroyed by Japanese porn. We have those 1970s soft-core porn movies made the Shaw brothers, but that style seems to be gone also.

(M3) There are so many funny pornographic games that are traded online, like a gay one where a young intern has to seduce all his superiors in order to get a promotion. And once I found this local production *Special Sperm Task Force,* a parody of the cartoon *X-Men*. It is like this movie that came out of nowhere, and I think it became like a cult movie.

(M4) I have been checking out the website of this Taiwanese guy, cumcruise.org, who made his own website. It has all these naked pictures of himself as he is traveling across the globe. I know that he got shut down by the Taiwanese government for some time, as he does not show full nudity anymore, but I like to check out his new galleries. I also go to Xtube sometimes to see if there are any Chinese men posting pictures, and once I found one video of a guy masturbating. I got all excited about it as I could see a Hong Kong taxicab in the background.

When interviewing women about their knowledge of DIY porn culture, they are, overall, supportive of the development. They do not have concrete knowledge about the actual web sites, nor can they imagine that they would be active downloaders or uploaders, but they do support other people's desires to participate. They support this development for three different reasons. First of all, they believe that watching some of these videos could have positive educational benefits. Second, they believe that these practices could be positive for sexual relationships. Third, they want to support DIY porn as a matter of civil liberties for those people who wish to openly express their sexual identities:

(F1) I think that they should have the freedom. We should not judge whether it is right or wrong, because it is just their freedom of expression. I think it is still fine if they post it on a porn forum, but if they go in a public website, without realizing that people under 18 could watch it and without giving a warning, then it is wrong.

(F2) I think they are normal and open channels for us to know more about others' personal lives. We can learn from those DIY videos. We can start to think about the relationship between sex and love. I used to think that think sex was something separate from love maybe, that if we have love we do not need to have sex. But nowadays, I think maybe sex can be related to love and maybe sometimes it can make two people become more intimate or more close to each other.

Men are supportive of DIY porn and they are more inclined to want to participate:

[M1] The first time that I saw these kinds of DIY pictures, I felt kind of surprised, that people would like to show their sex life and share with others. But when I saw a lot I did not feel surprised anymore. When I saw the Edison Chen's pictures, I was very surprised just because he is a star. I also sent these pictures to my girlfriend to watch. Maybe I would even like to take some pictures with her like that, but one has to very careful. But if you do not show your face, I think that it would be absolutely OK. This are very, very personal things, it is sex, so for me I won't share this kind of picture with my face.

[M2] I would say that DIY porn will be much more popular, yes because these years I have seen a lot of it. I heard a lot of discussions about these movies. It seems to be a trend for people begin to make these DIY porns. I think maybe they have watched too much commercial porn so maybe they want to do it themselves. Maybe they are bored with watching porn, they want to see the real thing.

Both women and men check out the pictures and videos from Internet leaks of celebrity's private sexual images and the related news incidents.

Conclusion

The central question in this chapter is how Chinese young adults are experiencing sexually explicit media as part of a social rebellion or a will to knowledge. The secondary question is how women and men embark on this sexual mutiny in different kind of ways. We thus interviewed a group of students about these questions and asked them to formulate how they get excited and educated by means of sexually explicit materials.

The differences between male and female arousal have mostly been discussed by clinical psychologists rather than cultural theorists. Western sexologists have found that female pornography consumption and arousal is open-ended and women react well to a wide range of sexual scenes, genres and orientations. Women prefer sexual diversity while men favor a particular genre or type of porn.

These findings are more pragmatically oriented as they focus on individual notions of arousal, rather than venturing into feminist arguments about sex culture. In our study, we try to interpret fe/male desires as part of social movements and specific cultural histories. Our study corrects the historical misconception that women have problems with sexual appetite and are uninterested in pornography. It is shown that they have different modes and ways of desiring and consuming porn and products with sexual content.

Women frame their viewing experiences as sex education and a quest for civil liberties. They want to participate in debates about sex activism and express a desire for alternatives to the products of mainstream pornography. Moreover, they want quality stories of eroticism with interesting backgrounds and scenarios that reflect their own feelings and relationships. Hence, their knowledge of digital media and eroticism is embedded in a search for social connections and intimacy. The male romance with pornography is more down to earth and consists of a daily search for coveted materials. Men take their porn collections for granted and they amass content excessively. As one male responded to our question "Do you often forward porn images to your friends?" Answer: "No, because I know that they are already overloaded." Men share plenty of materials with their male (net)friends and they also express a tentative desire to share images with their female friends or girlfriends. For women these images are dull and repulsive if not integrated into a more active expression of lust and social awareness.

Women sneak around the products of traditional male domains and feel the emotional glow of oddities and taboo images. The female porn experience produces contradictory feelings of repulsion and liberation. As Venus explained in an interview about her wavering porn tastes, when she was at a young age she was intrigued by many types of Japanese videos that had been forwarded by female friends. Some of them were shocking, like one video showing a men pleasuring a woman's anal region with tiny little eels. Those images were branded in her mind but also stirred her up to look for different scenes and movies, until she found what she was looking for. Additionally, women want pornography to keep abreast of news items about celebrities and their sex lives.

While many women see the porn experience as a mostly male phenomenon, they do want to be casually exposed to it and also want to support it for political reasons. We can see from our survey and interviews that Chinese women are reinventing sexual subjectivities around pornography, even though there has not yet been a cultural movement or niche industry to, potentially, suit their tastes. These wavering desires are not innate, nor uniquely Chinese, but they reflect the fact that young women are more assertive and will have a powerful voice in defining the sexual psychology and pleasures of the Internet generation.

Notes

1. For a full overview of tabloid media coverage and audience surveys of the Edison Chen sex scandal see the website http://www.zonaeuropa.com/200802b.brief.htm#007 (accessed 13 July 2011)

References

Chivers, Meredith, Rieger, Gerulf, Latty, Elizabeth and Bailey, Michael (2004) "A Sex Difference in the Specificity of Sexual Arousal," *Psychological Science,* 4: 11 pp. 736–44.

Chun, Wendy (2006) *Control and Freedom: Power and Paranoia in The Age of Fiber optics,* Cambridge, MA: MIT Press.

Foucault, Michel (1990) *A History of Sexuality, Vol. 1: And Introduction,* London: Vintage.

Ho, Sik-Ying and Tsang, K.T. (2006) "The Things Girls Shouldn't See: Relocating The Penis in Sex Education in Hong Kong," *Sex Education* 2: 1, pp. 61–73.

Jacobs, Katrien (2007) *Netporn: DIY Web Culture and Sexual Politics* Lanham MD: Rowman and Littlefield.

Janssen, Erick, Carpenter, Deanna and Graham, Cynthia A. (2003) "Selecting Films for Sex Research: Gender Differences in Erotic Film Preference," *Archives of Sexual Behavior,* 32: 3, pp. 243–51.

Kipnis, Laura (1996) *Bound and Gagged: Pornography and the Politics of Fantasy in America,* New York: Grove.

Mowlabocus, Sharif (2010) "Porn 2.0? Technology, Social Practice, and the New Online Porn Industry," in Feona Attwod (ed) *Porn.com. Making Sense of Online Pornography,* New York: Peter Lang, pp. 69–88.

Pei Yuxin, Ho Sik-Ying and Man Lun Ng (2007) "Studies on Women's Sexuality in China since 1980: A Critical Review," *Journal of Sex Research,* 2007, 44: 2, pp. 202–12.

Pei, Yuxin and Ho Sik-Ying (2009) "Gender, Self and Pleasure; Young Women's Discourses on Masturbation in Contemporary Shanghai," *Culture, Health, and Sexuality,* 1: 5, pp. 515–28.

Smith, Clarissa (2007) *One for the Girls: The Pleasures and Practices of Reading Women's Porn,* Bristol, UK: Intellect.

Chapter 4

Lizzy Kinsey and the Adult FriendFinders: An Ethnographic Case Study about Internet Sex and Pornographic Self-Display in Hong Kong

Introduction

The fourth chapter investigates web users, their sexual escapades and self-representations as observed on the sex and dating site http://www.adultfriendfinder.com (hereafter AFF.com). The website is a massive social network and pay site for people to upload DIY sex images and to find real-life partners for sex – whether it be for casual sex affairs between singles, swinging couples, or extra-marital affairs between "aba" (attached but available) individuals and their lovers. The chapter analyzes the imaging strategies of the Adult Friendfinders in reference to a playful adoption of commonplace notions of sexiness as "cybertypes." An online personality was created that would suit the goals and philosophy of AFF.com, while allowing the author to explore sexual self-display(具有性意味的自我展示) and the cultural context surrounding the website.

The materials presented here are based on a two-year case study carried out in Hong Kong. The words, fantasies and imaging choices of web users are extensively quoted, though they wish to remain anonymous in the context of this study. Some of my interlocutors were willing to answer my questions through chat or email exchanges, while others were interested in a face-to-face meeting. I arranged these meetings in public spaces such as restaurants or city parks. In most cases, I tried to have sincere and pleasant encounters and interviewed people a few times while alternating the interviewing environment. I also made efforts to socialize and relax with people outside these sessions by having lunch or dinner beforehand or afterwards.

My interviewing process, ideally, consisted of three phases. First of all, I asked people to explain and evaluate their acts of securing sex partners within the AFF.com web site. Second, I asked them to talk about sex culture in Hong Kong and how they believed the web site was making a difference for Chinese and non-Chinese people. Third, in some cases I asked people to tell me a sex story about one of their more eventful encounters. I asked in advance if I could record these conversations by means of audio or video recording, and some people gave me permission to do so. I tried to maintain a comfortable "soft" and "warm" atmosphere for culling sensitive information.

In my analysis of online exchanges and face-to-face encounters with Adult Friendfinders, I wanted to find out why culturally diverse women and men in Hong Kong had decided to use this US-based corporate network to seduce each other. People were adopting the site's sexualized personas and simplified pornographic identities as "cybertypes." What were their cultural associations with these identities, and how had the cultural encounters been stimulating for them? I also wondered whether the site privileged or hampered participants in the dating game depending on their racial profiles or their personalities.

My study was restricted to people who use the site for arranging non-commercial sexual encounters, though it is also used by sex workers to attract customers. For instance, a 40-year-old Asian woman, "Poppy Nipple", only shows interest in erotic chat and email and explains in her detailed profile that she works as a model for nude photography. Her language is very sexually charged and her profile picture shows a sexy lingerie outfit from the waist down. She writes that she is not a sex worker and is interested in using the site to develop online sex chats, though it is very unclear what her actual motivations are. Even though the website hosts such overlapping work/play identities, as direct sex work profiles would be forbidden, the online strategies of sex workers fall beyond the scope of this chapter. I wish to focus on "legitimate" AFF.com membership and the social flows of desire and its interracial inclinations.

DIY Pornography: Living and Breathing with Cybertypes.

AFF.com is run by a corporate-driven American entertainment company Friendfinder Networks Inc. It is one of the commercial giants of sexual entertainment and has now become involved in an ongoing trend towards Internet sexuality as participatory digital media or DIY pornography (自制色情内容). This trend involves a blurring between selfhood and the ephemeral signs, myths, and pathways of netporn culture (Jacobs 2007). Web users across the globe are encouraged to upload "pornographic identities" and write invitations to get access to other people's databases and eventually arrange sex dates.

Friendfinder Networks Inc. was founded in 1996 by a Silicon Valley company called Various that pioneered a variety of sex and dating sites. In December 2007 the site was sold for a groundbreaking US$500 million to Penthouse which was then making a successful adjustment from mainstream soft-core pornographic media to DIY pornography – the era of user-generated content and social networking. It thus became the world's largest corporate network for adult entertainment, owning and maintaining a booming family of sex sites with a combined membership of more than forty million users. The network caters to a wide range of cultures and communities based on various demographics such as age: seniorfinder. com, religion: BigChurch.com, JewishFriendfinder.com; and ethnicity or nationality: AsiaFriendfinder.com, IndianFriendfinder.com, Amigos.com, GermanFriendfinder.com, FrenchFriendfinder.com, KoreanFriendfinder.com, and FilipinoFriendfinder.com. These websites promise endless possibilities for inclusive and imaginative self-display and sexual joy; but do they really help people experience stimulating encounters within the sex culture of Hong Kong?

Although there are in theory very few restrictions on the kinds of sexy pictures and videos Hong Kong people can exchange, their choices are affected by engrained cultural behaviors, local social lifestyles and normative preaching by the expansionist corporate site itself.

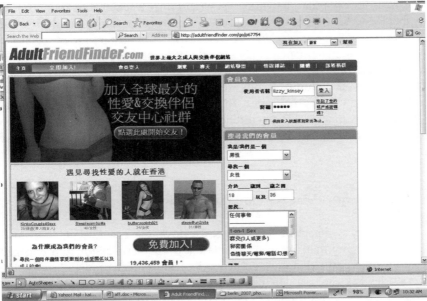

Figure 1: Screenshots of the Hong Kong site of Adult Friendfinder.com in both the English and Chinese language. Even though the website caters to a Chinese membership, the Caucasian "babes around the corner" dominate the photography galleries.

One of the projected behaviors on AFF.com seems to be an assumed familiarity with pornographic clichés of gender and race; or a collective use of generic and predictable names, images and profiles. Lisa Nakamura has pointed out in *Cybertypes: Race, Ethnicity and Identity on the Internet* that digital networks are socially-transformative spaces precisely in how they allow people to play with stereotyped depictions of race and gender within emerging media cultures (Nakamura 2002: 5). It is hard to pinpoint who the perpetrators of the old racist stereotypes are, as web users collaborate in creating the semantics of a new. Nakamura is interested in how racial identity, racial diversity and racist attitudes are engendered in machine-enabled communication practices and believes that "cybertyping" performs a crucial role within the signifying practices of networks.

Even though this analysis of AFF.com is not primarily focused on race and racial identity, it applies Nakamura's philosophical approach to studying self-display. People may decide to disguise themselves as "types" in order to maximize their chances at finding partners, though these signifying practices would obviously be hurtful and off-putting to potential partners. I wanted to find out what the more complex inter-cultural probings and frustrations were for people who were using the site. Disguised as Lizzy Kinsey, I wanted to get involved in this massive network and witness its spaces of transgression as well as its pitfalls and boundaries. For my research I used the example and model of Danah Boyd (2007), who has equally functioned as a participant and ethnographerof the social networks MySpace and Facebook in order to witness and document deep-rooted social divisions (社會分化) amongst US teens. Her study reveals how popular networks easily reproduce a social elitism or ethos of upward mobility that leaves behind the imaging processes of fringe or minority cultures. The self-representations of Hong Kong sex seekers are read against this background of social and racial unrest within a potentially-emancipatory sex site. Web users exploit social networks because they want to parade and display their subjectivities and social connections (Donath and Boyd 2004: 72). As players within AFF.com, web users show themselves and their social circles as sexual beings and cybersexual types. Through my interactions with AFF.com as "Lizzy Kinsey, scholarly sex machine," I acted diligently and emphatically to find my own answers and sexual connections, while inviting web users to cooperate in generating a unique kind of reflection.

The Lizzy Kinsey Online Experiment as Auto-Ethnography

In developing a theoretical perspective on Lizzy Kinsey's online experiment, this study contributes to an ethnography that can accommodate a deeper immersion and engaged performativity within different media environments. Ken Plummer's model of garnering and dissecting sex stories was also useful in that it allowed for strategies of emotive-relational bonding (Plummer 1995: XI). Additionally, I was guided by artists-scholars who shared scholarly reflections arising from immersion in sex sites. Chantal Zakari's book *webAffairs*, an artist's documentary of an adult video web community, helped me experience sexual attraction as aesthetic experiences within mass media environments (Zakari nd). Isaac Leung is a Hong Kong artist/scholar who took on the identity of 'Japan boy' to investigate power relations within gay cyber sex sites. In his project, 'The Impossibility of Having Sex with 500 Men in a Month – I'm an Oriental Whore,' he detailed his journey into sexual bliss and orgasm and its ensuing limitations and frustrations (Leung nd).

For my own study, I created the profile of a scholarly sex machine in order to attract people and to negotiate a sexual-intellectual kind of cooperation. At first, people started sharing sexual testimonies and fantasy stories as a form of symbolic interaction and cultural commentary. At a second stage, I asked several people to enter a public space and begin a dialogue about Internet sex. In order to process these encounters, I became interested in mixing the genres of diary writing and academic analysis. This type of ethnographic enquiry has been associated with female or feminist writers and their attempts to maintain empathic and reflective voices to facilitate social knowledge and intimacy (Reed-Danayah 1997: 16).

In August 2006, I uploaded the profile of Lizzy Kinsey, a 40-year-old Caucasian bi-sexual woman, who is the imagined granddaughter of American sexologist Alfred Kinsey. Alongside

Figure 2: The profile picture of Lizzy Kinsey used on AFF.com to attract members and engage in dialogue.

my scholarly ambitions to garner data and interview people, I wanted to experiment with my own sexual self-display. I wanted to attract web users by photographing and displaying my naked body, while also dropping hints with regards to my underlying research goals. The picture I selected shows a close-up of my naked torso and breasts, while sitting down on my knees with a pen lying on top of my legs. I have scribbled a written text on my stomach that reads "Are you Ready?" Lizzy Kinsey was cast as an outgoing and sexually-active female who uses a pen as a reflective tool. The pen could be seen as an instrument to play with sexually or to record stories. Lastly, I followed the AFF.com fashion of the day and disguised my identity by cropping the picture and not showing my face. Hence I had created my own "cybertype" that could be easily accepted within the network but was also a disguise that could be dismantled by my interlocutors.

In the written part of the profile, people were asked to send me their erotic secrets and stories, or to share experiences in a face-to-face encounter. The response was overwhelming as Lizzy Kinsey received five to six sexual invitations on a daily basis. I rewrote the profile a couple of times but it was always generic so that people would have to guess about the underlying motivations. By using this particular profile, I attracted and teased people who were interested in sex and in picking me up or chatting online. I slowly revealed to them that I was a researcher who wanted to share and record their stories and experiences. Many people simply disappeared at that point, or they masturbated their way through these negotiations and then dropped off, but some remained on board and were willing to share more in-depth information.

I had extensive correspondences with about twenty people and conducted interviews with them either by email or through face-to-face meetings. I have selectively quoted from three of these interviews to highlight the cross-cultural dating environment. The second reason for quoting from these peculiar dialogues has to do with the focus of this chapter, which is a personalized and emotionally-engaged analysis of cross-racial encounters as (auto) ethnography.

The profile of Lizzy Kinsey allowed me to explore the website and make use of my sexual body while attracting people who would help me along in my intellectual pursuit. I also used it as a tool to reflect on my own boundary-crossing experiment and to test out collective self-objectifying impulses within Internet sex culture. Through my profile I triggered people's fantasies and desires and explored an unusual experiment at gathering social-sexual knowledge. It produced sparkling insights, but they were indeed often ephemeral and did not always lead to further contact. I was unable to get more significant insights from a large number of people who gradually dropped out, though their daily responses became a legitimate force in the ongoing experiment as a way to explore dating rituals. A more diversified research team would no doubt have observed other aspects based on their own specific cultural backgrounds and their varying degrees of willingness to participate.

The Sex Rituals of Adult FriendFinders in Hong Kong

AFF.com is primarily a site for heterosexual sex and dating activities, where people share pictures and movies via web portals in an attempt to seduce others into sexual encounters. Members use the web site for daily browsing and to build a somewhat loyal network of friends. Even though the site spreads a promotional rhetoric of browsing for sex with instant results, as indicated by its slogan: "meet real sex partners tonight! (今夜就遇見真正的性愛夥伴！)", it is also a virtual lounge with other services and distractions for those who are stuck at home. People use the site to upload and tweak their profiles, to conduct live chats with remote or anonymous partners, to spy on photographs and video albums, or play silly games such as the Wet T-shirt Contest and the Naughty Carol Contest.

Every time an AFF member is contacted by another member, a happy upbeat announcement is sent to their private email account. In addition, AFF.com sends out a daily deluge of ads to its members, who easily receive a daily average of four to five ads. The match-making engine is unrelenting and uses all its automated skills to encourage members to use various applications which will lead to them having sex. It is like a nagging friend who worries for your sexual well-being and wants you to go on a date as soon as possible. Members are given three to four encouraging messages every day, containing lists and thumbnail photographs of other members who have already contacted them, members who live in their vicinity and are ready for action, or members who match their profile. The network uses a pushy "you need to get laid (你需要上床)" or "you are ready!(你已經準備好了)" rhetoric everywhere, even though such rhetoric would be clearly out of place or undesirable within a wide range of social circles. The site simply displays a lack of sensitivity towards the diverse demographics it is hoping to attract.

Moreover, the site pretends to be a potentially-enormous sex aid for female and male users across different cultural regions and demographics, but it actually does not show any knowledge about gender or cultural differences. For instance, the site has invited Internet pornography companies to place advertising and to offer video-on-demand selections, but these do not cater to Asian customers. When opening the Hong Kong site in either English or Chinese, there is an abundant amount of American porn (美式色情片) and Caucasian models (白種模特). The site also selects five to six naked pictures of female Caucasians within the AFF community to lure other members. Very few attempts are made to include ethnic diversity or to offer male top model teasers for female tastes.

In December 2007 there were about 100,000 male members in Hong Kong versus 8,000 females. This uneven gender ratio is similar in most of the sites in other cultures, as there currently is a shortage of women who want to sign up. As a result of the uneven gender ratio, women who open profiles are automatically swamped with requests, while males may be starved for a reply for weeks on end. In Hong Kong the site is now available in Chinese and in English, but web users from Chinese and non-Chinese backgrounds mostly correspond with each other in English. This is probably due to the fact that the Hong Kong site, from its inception, has failed to attract the Cantonese-speaking cultural majority. Rather, it has attracted web users from several ethnic and linguistic backgrounds who all correspond in English. The site became very popular around 2005 and has continued to expand its membership. It had 60,000 members when I started my research in August 2006 and almost tripled its membership by the time I ended it in August 2008. Other cultures with a population size close to Hong Kong have attracted a larger membership, but the Hong Kong website has nonetheless gained a substantial group of web users who actively upload content and pursue sex.

The site is a novel phenomenon in Hong Kong, where people are not encouraged to pursue sexualized self-representation or explore DIY porn environments as people have in Western cultures. As sexologist Dr. Man Lune Ng explains, Hong Kong is a sophisticated and Western-influenced metropolis with a high-tech infrastructure and diverse web communities, but there are severe undercurrents of moral and social conservatism. Hong Kong's progressive communities and sex activists strive towards a healthier cultural climate, including freedom of speech and basic sexual rights. At the same time sex activism is hampered by intolerant attitudes and by mainland China's war on pornography and its Internet censorship. Dr. Ng also observes that a clear sexual split is found in Hong Kong sex culture as the Chinese and Western mindsets often vigorously clash with each other. (Ng Man Lune 2006) These historically-embedded tensions within Hong Kong's post-colonial society contribute to a

Figure 3: Profile pictures of "male member" on AFF.com. Many members crop or digitally erase their face and have taken the habit of uploading a picture of their penis.

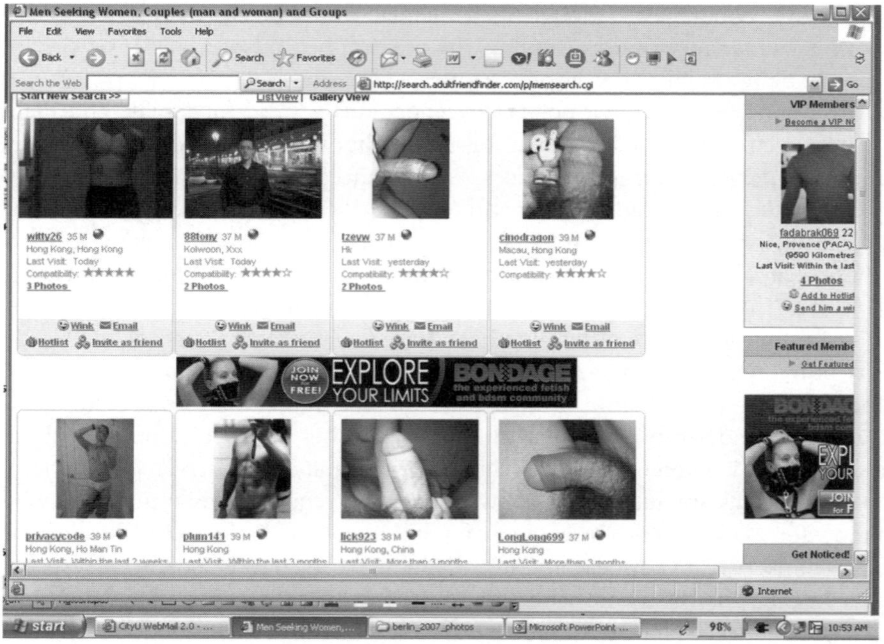

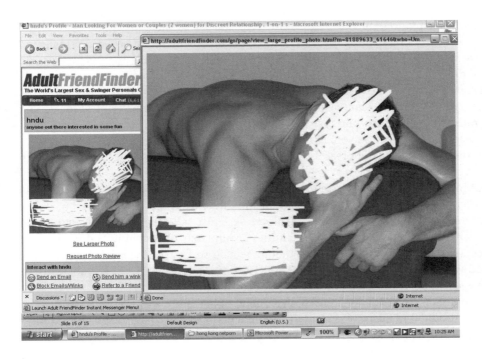

heightened atmosphere of anger and frustration amongst web users who are trying out a new multi-cultural environment.

I wanted to find out who the cultural winners and losers were amongst the Internet hunters in Hong Kong. Since the Chinese male majority is underrepresented, there is indeed more room for non-Chinese males to attract women. The site has certainly attracted a large percentage of Caucasian males who use the site to hook up with Chinese women. Chinese women have taken advantage of this situation to test out cross-racial dating and cater their profiles to non-Chinese males. In order to understand this model of cross-racial desire, one could attempt a comparison with Karen Kelsky's analysis of Japanese women and their romantic fantasies about foreigners or cosmopolitan culture. Hong Kong women seem to favor or romanticize the "foreign" status and sex appeal of the site to resist gendered expectations within the local culture. (Kelsky 2001: 2) At the same time, as will be shown in more detail later, they use commonplace notions of sexualized femininity to cater to male users.

Searching through a collection of Asian females who use English to seduce others, but whose mother tongue is Cantonese or Mandarin, we detect a wide range of names and personas associated with "whore-like" or "bad girl" femininity (妓女或壞女孩式的女性特質). In most cases the chosen names refer to universally sexy types and do not have any reference to ethnicity, such as "Exotic Allure," "Naughty Mommy," "Daily Diva," "Wicked Angel" and "Sexy Bitch." However, in about 30 per cent of the cases, women include various ethnic labels, such as "HKWifey," "SakuraHK, "HK Lulu," "Your China Lover" or "Gloomy China." For their photographs, females mostly use images of their nude bodies or close-up pictures of their breasts, legs, buttocks, or vaginas. The difference between female and male profiles is that women use a larger variety of body parts, while males largely use a picture of their erect penis. In the case of heterosexual swinging couples, the naked body of the female partner is often chosen to represent the couple. For instance, a 50-year-old interracial Asian-Caucasian couple approached Lizzy Kinsey with this request for action: "We are more than ready. I would love to write on your body with my tongue and we could trace some interesting lines on you. Do drop us a line." The profile image used by this couple is that of the Asian's woman's breasts, and they use this image to hide a fuller identity in order to maximize their chances at sexual seduction.

The Chinese female profiles establish a reversal of normative depictions of Chinese women as either well-behaved, good girls, or passive and pleasantly-subdued bed partners. These reversals support the findings of Chinese feminist scholars who have found that women increasingly articulate positive identities around acts of watching and consuming sex images (Ho and Tsang 2006 71). Even though female erotic cybertypes are accepted and applauded within the cultural context of Adult Friendfinder, they are still at odds with, or rebelling against, the traditional patriarchal sex culture of Hong Kong.

Male profiles on AFF.com are focused on a potent sexual body, including a picture of the erect cock. About 50 per cent of males who approached Lizzy used an image of their erect penis. Additionally, people used clichéd names like "EndlessFun," "HK juicy lover," "Black," or "HK_puppy_dog." These choices can be seen as unimaginative in selling a phallic male ego, but it is important to note that men from diverse backgrounds participate in this trend and thus deconstruct of the idea of the ideal penis. One could indeed applaud this trend towards autonomy and diversification because it allows men to participate in definitions of sexuality and sexual pride (Lehman 2007: 111). Watching sexually explicit images can evoke powerful emotions and stir people to make changes in their private lives. These crude home-made images of private genitals are arguably even more powerful as they allow the subject to "become" those bodily zones that are typically censored. Nonetheless, the dominance of a phallic images also reinforce a "crude male force" that wants to get satisfaction. Even though they cast the keen male genital in various shapes, sizes and skin colors, they also simply echo the "We all need to get laid here" rhetoric of the AFF.com ad campaigns. When looking through these profiles, I was overcome with a wide range of emotions, but I rarely got sexually stimulated or aesthetically awed by them. This was partially due to the fact that I tried to have some emotional distance as a researcher, but it also meant that I simply failed to get stimulated by these images on a deeper level.

Face-to-Face Meetings with Cybertypes

Adult FriendFinder is an expansionist business venture trying to sell the image of a euphoric sex hunter who finds his/her prey regardless of social divisions and backgrounds. The website uses aggressive ad campaigns to convince web users to improve their technological competencies and learn how to upload and fine-tune suitably sexy profiles. Web users have internalized this rhetoric through self-objectification and the use of clichés, which can function as a useful mask within the online sex zone. The generic profiles of sexuality can be easily manipulated, fine-tuned or deleted on a website, but how do they cling to us as social agents within the Hong Kong sex environment?

Nakamura explains that one cannot just employ online personas without tapping into personal histories and cultural experiences of ethnic and social groups. Just as Nakamura theorizes cybertypes to reveal social and racial anxieties, I wanted to examine human stories and complexities behind the use of a mask. I interacted with the women of the profile "Double Trouble" – two Chinese women who also call themselves Nin and Ning. Their profile read as follows:

We welcome overseas applicants, Caucasians only ... For those who have short concentration span: All emails without a recent face pic and cock size will be banned immediately ... Ning has 34D bra size and her nipples of course are delicious. She is 5′2″ and has the smoothest white skin. She hates being spanked! Nin is the naughty younger sister, 30 years old. She is 5′6″, has small tits, keen nipples and a nice tan. She loves being spanked during doggy.

Ning and Nin both love young hot white guys between 25 and 38, but who are not young at heart. They must be "athletic and very tall and they must not have saggy asses." They specify that the penis they were looking for has to be a "Rock hard average cock (hump the magic seven …): 7 inches. Not too thick as we both have tight pussies. We will update our profile accordingly if they want to venture into huge black cocks or nine inchers."

The tone of the profile was indeed humorous and included a pictorial comparison between the bodies of Nin and Ning. But the profile also included those typical references to ethnic categories and body types that could be off-putting or offensive to many potential candidates. Why did they use these references and how were members responding? I first met face-to-face with Nin in a restaurant where she was very friendly and generous, but her partner Ning had decided not to participate in the study. We talked about interracial dating and she told me that many local girls still dream about dating foreigners. We had an email exchange a few days later and the tone of her messages was humorous and witty, as we were both acting out our bad girl personas. She explained that she developed the "Double Trouble" identity primarily to cater to male fantasies, but it had indeed started to affect her sexual preferences. As a matter of fact, she was eager to discuss her boundary-crossing experiences and this is how we were able to bond on an emotional level.

I asked her about her relationship with Ning and why she had decided to team up with another female. Nin replied: "We aren't lovers in real life. We have touched and kissed each other but that's it. No oral sex or hand jobs between us." She explained later that she believes that most women have a more fluid sexuality than men. Even though she did not think of herself as a bi-sexual woman, she still enjoyed observing her female partner. In the second interview, Nin clarified that she got turned on by seeing her friend having sex with a man because she could imagine what he would do to her.

Several weeks later, I conducted an in-depth interview while she sat at a computer and explained how she browses profiles and uses the website. She was projecting a different type of mood and personality and indicated that she actually did not like most of the male profiles on AFF.com and was looking for a deeper connection. When I pointed to the racial descriptions in her profile and asked her why she did not like Chinese men, she denied having a racial preference and brought it down to the issue of penis size:

I don't have a racial preference but I do like men who are tall and relatively well-endowed (around 6.5 to 7 inches) so most of the guys I date are Caucasians. Of course not all Caucasians are well-endowed but on average they are slightly bigger/thicker than Asian men. I have not been out with a black man yet. I haven't been approached by one in real life … I found out many women on the site (either from their blogs or their comments on others' blogs) say size does not matter, but I disagree. I can feel the difference between having a 6-inch and 7-inch cock. I do like slightly bigger one but 8 inches are my maximum. Before I joined the site, I thought 6 inches was a below average size for white men but it turns out they are average.

Nin later confirmed that she preferred Caucasians because Asian men have smaller penises, and she even added that she thinks Indians are an exception and have slightly bigger penises. When I recalled her remarks about penis size and racial preference, she then qualified her attitude by pointing to historical-cultural factors:

> I think it's also a historical problem. Some people tend to think white men are better in bed because they are more experienced. They know how to please women, etcetera. But you also have to consider the fact that all the expats have their own apartment but local men do not. How often can you have sex if you do not have your own place? It's bound to be difficult, isn't it? I also wonder if there are Chinese women who think it is OK to be promiscuous or sexually open in front of white men but not in front of Asian men, especially those who think they will marry an Asian man in the end.

Nin added that her attraction to Caucasians had something to do with the movies that she grew up with, the education she received and her major in English literature. She showed that her desire for Caucasian males grew out of complex individual desires and historical factors and that she ultimately acts out clichés to her own benefit. Her persona of a "bad girl with opportunistic taste" allowed her to easily control AFF traffic while hiding the more vulnerable or socially-conformist layers of her personality. She used the profile to have a higher success rate on this cross-cultural dating ground, while trespassing local cultural restrictions about lustful femininity and alternative sex.

Kelsky (2001) has observed that the desire of Japanese women to avoid the traps of local culture may reinforce the traditional relations of power they appear to be undermining. The rebellious bad girl who dates "Caucasians only" is equally an example of a racist slur. "Double Trouble" was obviously trying to play it both ways by adopting a juicy label within the AFF community, while trampling on the norms of traditional Chinese culture and offending a large portion of the male population.

In order to find out how males were adopting and reacting to cybertypes, I also had face-to-face interviews with several AFF.com males. The first one who agreed to be interviewed was Damon Lust, a Caucasian male in his late thirties who had lived in Hong Kong for several years. He was the person who actually told me about the popularity of the AFF.com site. He was aware of the fact that I was a researcher and also wanted to wish me well on a personal level. He talked to me extensively about his sex encounters as we became friends and shared our thoughts.

I mostly talked to him about his relations with Chinese women and couples. Damon confirmed that there was indeed a lot of traffic between Caucasian males and Chinese females on AFF.com. He was very interested in meeting Chinese females who wanted to target foreigners like him. He had created a profile to suit interracial desires, describing himself as "a very handsome, sexual and highly-cultured foreigner interested in local dates." Damon was also eager to help me analyze the culture of the site in general and provided further insights about social class and power relations:

There is a Chinese revolution of sorts going on at this site, but it is a female revolution. The Chinese men do not seem that interested, even though many of them have extra-marital affairs by visiting sex workers or taking on mistresses from mainland China. The *gwailo* population like myself takes advantage of this situation as there are a high number of sex-starved Chinese women who are relatively easy to get. But there is some kind of revolution in that these women are starting to take control of this situation and take pleasure in it, by talking about it and showing it off. They have more lovers than you think they do. And of course the Internet has made it much easier for these women to participate. You'd be surprised to see how many respectable women are actually out there.

It became clear that the opportunistic bad girl type was influencing social relations within AFF.com community and allowing Chinese women to control traffic by attracting or rejecting foreigners. Damon confirmed that women acted out bossy personas in order to seduce him. When he had just signed up to AFF.com, he tried to meet with one of the sexually-forward Chinese women who wrote him that "she was in a gangbang mood." However he did not have any naked pictures of himself at that moment, so he lost his chance as she demanded to see a picture. He also told me that he got rejected in the same way by "Double Trouble."

Even though AFF.com requires a membership, Damon believes that overall it has had a democratizing effect in Hong Kong society. He himself was able to go out with Chinese and Caucasian people from very different class backgrounds. He saw a clear difference between an AFF.com class and the traditional high-society or cosmopolitan class of Hong Kong. As he explained:

The site is perhaps still expat-dominated but it is very different from the social upper crust of Hong Kong. Hong Kong is a very money-driven city, not just for those very rich people. The upper crust have sexual affairs with each other, but they really don't need the Internet or digital technologies. They have extremely high-class prostitution and escort networks. The large presence of male Caucasians shows that the business class in Hong Kong is now using Internet sex to arrange casual affairs, when in previous times they may have resorted to entertainment with commercial sex workers.

I also conducted several interviews with Pong Leung, a 44-year-old Chinese male and sports instructor who wanted to share ideas about power relations and social class. He used the name of an American celebrity in his profile and added pictures of his well-developed back muscles. He did not mind meeting me for face-to-face interviews and told me that he had on-and-off experiences with Internet dating for over ten years. Indeed, he had sent me a message on AFF.com saying that he wanted to have sex with a blonde. I asked him where he got that idea, and he replied:

Hello Dear, Well, I am a local Hong Kong-er who wants to have sex with a Western lady. When I was young, I watched Charlie's Angels (the very 1st version). I was totally attracted by the gals … Kate Jackson, Jacqueline Smith and the blonde … In my mind, I believe the blonde is the most beautiful creature in the world. So, I would love to have sex with a blonde … And I work hard on my English … build up my body … hoping that one day I will have sex with a blonde … so, please write to me, see what will happen. We may go swimming, enjoy sunbathing … enjoy a lazy afternoon in a hotel room … Once again, write me back and let's have some fun.

Pong Leung turned out be a very friendly, shy and mellow person when we had our first lunch meeting. He insisted that I was a sexy person but was kind enough to stick to the ethnographic plot. He was quite insecure about his physical appearance and command of the English language. I invited Pong Leung for a second videotaped interview which took place while he browsed AFF.com. In this interview he told me about the difficulties he was experiencing in getting sex dates on the site. He showed fifteen profiles of Chinese women who stated that they wanted to only date Western guys or used the racist phrase "Caucasians only." He said that it did make him sad but that everybody should be entitled to their own taste. He was almost certain that he would not get any dates with Chinese women but was not really in despair. He was very interested in having casual sex affairs, but believed that he eventually might get married and would try to meet a steady partner through very different channels. He used the site to browse profiles and DIY photos of women who had captured his attention. He also wanted to terminate his membership as he had figured out that the race/power dynamic was directed against him.

Conclusion

This analysis of Hong Kong social dynamics and cybersex types is based on a longitudinal ethnographic case study where I gradually gathered stories and interviews by interacting with people online and in face-to-face encounters. These encounters were difficult to establish and developed only gradually, while I continuously observed the seduction games and imaging strategies of a massive social network. This case study highlights a group of cultural diverse women and men in Hong Kong, who are highly computer-literate and sexually-active individuals, and who help each other in constructing self-portraits and formulating new sexual identities. This chapter set out to find out why people wanted to explore this particular network for casual sex and DIY pornography and what their reasons were for adopting a specific type of self-display. Since I was personally involved and was hoping to find useful connections, I used my own masked identity and pornographic cybertype to gaze at others and to strike up conversations that became the raw data for this study.

Through participant observation and interviews, the study highlights that these types of profiles are collectively tested and endorsed. They are convenient and often humorous labels and provide an easy way for people to control subjectivity. Hong Kong sex seekers also adopt these cybertypes and their pedestrian, raunchy or racist connotations to create cosmopolitan subjectivities and escape from local biases against casual sex. The desire to escape into a foreign realm provides creative stimulation, but arguably reinforces a conservative-bourgeois cosmopolitanism rather than progressive sex culture (Kelsky 2001: 15).

Through my observations and dialogues I witnessed sexual euphoria and emancipation, as well as racial tensions and dismissive attitudes between men and women. It is interesting to note that Chinese women specifically use opportunistic profiles to attract foreigners, though they include elements of sexual excess to differentiate themselves within the local culture. As Lizzy Kinsey, I was investigating and playing with a desire to become part of this network, which to me also represents a realm of cross-racial desire that might possibly be used to transcend my local alienation. I constructed my own persona with a bad-girl flavor to be a sex machine on the site, yet situated myself as a rebel within the context of academic research. By connecting with people through my own cybertype, I could relate to their layered identities and wait for the deeper stories to be revealed.

Cyber sex identities and relationships historically have a lineage in non-sexual bonding such as chat rooms and online role-playing games. That is, web users first connect with each other as loyal and supportive online mates and they may then gradually develop a intimate relationship that results in sex or friendship (McKenna 2006: 121). If we place AFF.com within this lineage of online intimacy, we can see that its apparent mission, to arrange real-life sexual encounters based on minimum or no foreplay, is a novel approach to sex that would be uncomfortable to a wide range of people. In this sense, the AFF self-display strategies are totally different from those used by Hong Kong people on other dating sites or general social networks like MySpace and Facebook. People on general dating sites tend to write complex, lengthy and often idealized profiles that encapsulate their self-growth or the person they hope to be in future times (Ellison et al. 2006: 15). AFF.com members adopt curtailed identities as a convenient mask to hide behind while revealing pornographic selves and their attempts to cross boundaries. These strategies allow them to plunge into DIY porn, as the mask itself is endorsed by the community while appearing enigmatic, or indeed dumb, to the outside world. Nakamura shows that cybertypes are not as dumb as they might appear, but have a life-course with historically-embedded cultural expectations, and they therefore cannot be seen as fleeting data-entities. The goal of my personalized and selective approach to ethnography was to genuinely befriend people and to be able to look behind their mask. In doing so, I invited them to respond to my own desires and frustrations as a researcher in a journey of sexual and cultural discovery.

Note: A previous version of this article was published in *Culture, Health and Sexuality*, Vol 12, Issue 6, May 2010.

References

Boyd, Danah (2007) "Viewing American Class Divisions through Facebook and MySpace," *Danah Boyd Blog*, 24 June, http://www.danah.org/papers/essays/ClassDivisions.html (accessed 11 July 2011).

Donath, Judith and Boyd, D. (2004) "Public Displays of Connections," *BT Technology Journal*, 22: 4, pp. 71–82.

Ellison, Nicole, Heino, R. and Gibbs, J. (2006) "Managing Impressions Online: Self-Presentations Processes in the Online Dating Environment," *Journal of Computer-Mediated Communication*, 11: 2, pp. 1–24.

Ho, Sik-Ying and Tsang, K.T. (2006) "The Things Girls Shouldn't See: Relocating The Penis in Sex Education in Hong Kong," *Sex Education* 2: 1, pp. 61–73.

Jacobs, Katrien (2007) *Netporn: DIY Web Culture and Sexual Politics*, Lanham, MA: Rowman and Littlefield.

Kelsky, Karen (2001) *Women on the Verge: Japanese Women, Western Dreams*, Durham: Duke University Press.

Lehman, Peter (2007) "You and Voyeurweb: Illustrating the Shifting Representation of the Penis on Internet with User-Generated Content," *Cinema Journal* 46: 4, pp. 105–15.

Leung, Isaac (nd)"The Impossibility of Having Sex with 500 Men in a Month-I'm an Oriental Whore," http://isaacleung.com/orientalwhore/ (no longer available).

McKenna, Katelyn (2006) "A Progressive Affair: Online Dating to Real World Mating," in Monica T. Witty, Andrea J. Baker and James A. Inman (eds.), *Online matchmaking*, New York City: Palgrave (pp. 116–36).

Nakamura, Lisa (2002) *Cybertypes: Race, Ethnicity, and Identity on the Internet*, New York: Routledge.

Ng, Man Lune (2006) "Hong Kong. The International Encyclopedia of Sexuality at Humboldt University," http://www2.hu-berlin.de/sexology/IES/hongkong.html (accessed 12 July 2011).

Plummer, Ken (1995) *Telling Sexual Stories: Power, Change, and Social Worlds*, New York and London: Routledge.

Reed-Danahay, Deborah (ed) (1997) *Auto/Ethnography: Rewriting the Self and the Social*, UK Oxford: Berg.

Zakari, Chantal (nd) *webAffairs*, http://www.webaffairsbook.info/webAffairs1.html (accessed 11 July 2011).

Chapter 5

It Runs in the Rotten Family: Queer Love Amongst Animation Fans and Costume Players

Introduction

We continue our analysis of a mutinous tendency within Chinese sexually explicit media as they are surfacing within different pop cultures and media environments. This last chapter will discuss the importance of visual fantasy cultures and the virtual worlds of animation fans, costume players (Cosplay 扮裝角色扮演) and Gothic Lolita (哥特式洛麗塔) impersonators. These creators of virtual fantasy worlds exhibit multiple variations on queer sexuality that affect embodiment, desire and a sense of minority grouping within public culture. Their flamboyant appearances endorse practices of "eccentricity" and "abjection," which they carefully prepare and show off in gatherings and on the Internet. They also express oppositional viewpoints that question the demands of high consumerism and the patriarchal guidelines of the nation-state.

The "Cosplay zone" allows fans to explore a smooth and ambiguous kind of nonconformity as they model themselves on the stars and starlets of animation culture. Fans also follow certain "edgy" Japanese life-styles as an escape from the restrictions and stigmas within Chinese sex culture. The excessive knowledge and impersonation of these styles helps people generate fictions that suspend local social pressures and cultural constraints. It will be shown that the adoption of humanoid forms and animation characters is a new type of social-emotional bonding and collective intelligence.

Queer (酷兒) is originally an umbrella term for non-heteronormative expressions of gender and desires, including LGBT people (lesbian, gay, bisexuals, and transgender) and non-normative heterosexual people. Animation fans develop queer subjectivities based on fictionalized depictions of love and kinship. They have unique ways of acting out a wavering sexuality of transgression, an experience of identifying with rotating characters or multiple alter egos without ever becoming one of them.

A Spark Can Cause a Prairie Fire (星星之火可以燎原)

Costume play (角色扮演) has become a theatrical popular culture and global cultural trend amongst animation fans all over Asia, and beyond. Young adults dress up in themed costumes and assume the persona of characters from their favorite comic books (manga), animated cartoons (anime) and cute or gothic style Lolitas from Japanese and Korean ACG industries (Animation, Comics and Games) (動漫產業). Through their obsessive reading and devoted spectatorship, young people have started experiencing a blurring of "self" and "character" within visual fantasy cultures.

For instance, "Mizuki Mochizuki" is a fashion student at Hong Kong Polytechnic University (香港理工大學), who prefers to live out bygone centuries by dressing up as princess characters, such as the historical Princess Elisabeth from Hungary (Sisi) (茜茜公主) or Marie Antoinette (瑪麗皇后), a character found in the shojo manga *Rose of Versailles* (凡爾賽玫瑰). Mizuki is very articulate and passionate about the classics of Japanese animation and further channels her identity by relentlessly creating a self-made collection of elaborate costumes.

Mizuki and other animation lovers are in search of new identities and are invested in the products of global fashion and the cultural flows between the capital cities of Tokyo, Hong Kong, Taipei, Shanghai, and Beijing (Iwabuchi 2002). In Hong Kong, the globalization of Japanese animation styles started in the mid-1960s as local and mainland-trained artists copied Japanese styles and developed specific local versions, entitled "manhua" (漫畫) cartoons. Other countries such as China banned Japanese animation products, so product influx and social trends occurred initially via markets in Hong Kong (Wong 2006).

Figure 1: Cosplayer Mizuki Mochizuki dressing up as Queen Marie Antoinette from the Manga classic, *Rose of Versailles*. This is one of a dozen characters that define her identity as a Cosplayer.

From the early days of Japanese ACG importation, Chinese audiences have devoured the audio-visual aesthetics and love lives of beautiful animation characters. Some fans have developed attachments to queer niche-genres such as yaoi (矢追) or Boy Love (耽美), which depicts male homosexual love stories catered to female readers. Others have used fantasy elements to rethink the boundaries between fantasy and physicality by acknowledging modes of cross-dressing. Japanese *Shojo* (young female) animation (少女漫畫) has made great efforts to propose fantasy-driven concepts of masculinity and femininity as a queer sexuality that offers escape from the roles and strictures of contemporary adult society (Orbaugh 2003). The gender-fluid characters represent a state of being that is socially unanchored, free of responsibility and highly self absorbed – the opposite of the ideal Japanese male or female adult.

Some of the Japanese critics in the late 1980s were worried about the *shojo* trend, arguing that it signified the downfall of Japanese culture, as both female and male consumers groups were adopting shallow, materialistic habits. Horikiri Naoto and Yamane Kazuma bemoaned the fact that the Japanese were increasingly prone to compulsory and excessive consumerism, and argued that the national character would become infantilized. The problem was no longer that the national character behaved like a middle-aged male in love with a much younger girl, but would be acting like the girl herself. The world *shojo* (young girl) culture thus came to signify "a state of consumerism, passivity, commodification, narcissism, consumption without production, moral and ethical emptiness, and self-referentiality" (Orbaugh 2003: 204).

My interest in "unanchored" love spaces and their queer kinship structures was first piqued by research into online marriage among animation fans in mainland China. One of the major Internet sites of that time, Animation Garden (動漫花園), encouraged fans to build family relationships while sharing the products of animation culture. In a specific area of the site, the Nongfu Mountain Forum (農夫山), half of its membership was "getting married." The site would issue a certificate after the marriage took place and members would display their marriage status in all of their correspondences. They would also upload a copy of their marriage certificate on the website:

結婚証號碼：花字 (2005) 00011號 Marriage Certificate

根據農夫山婚姻法，我在此宣布 wilfredsun 和 木棉草 成為夫妻。二人婚姻關系從即日起生效，受到花園法律的保護，享有因此而來的權利及承擔相應的義務。希望兩人相親相愛，白頭偕老。

According to Marriage Law, I announced that Wilfredsun and Mumiancao become couple now. Hope your love will last forever.

花園民事法官 Animation Garden Judge

kairi (簽名) Signature
2005年9月1日 Date

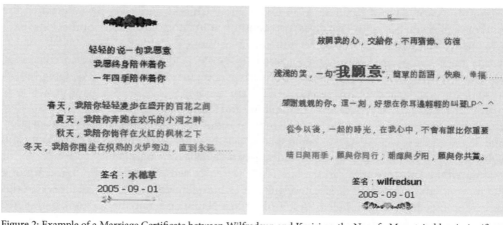

Figure 2: Example of a Marriage Certificate between Wilfredsun and Krairi on the Nongfu Mountain bbs. A significant number of members of this bbs tended to engage in virtual marriage; some of them also got divorced there.

At the same time, the institution of gay/lesbian marriage was being debated on the website.[1] Many animation fans seemed interested in queer pairings but the site's administrators eventually decided not to allow gay or lesbian marriage.

Members expressed excessive emotions and aspirations about their straight and queer virtual relationships when we interviewed them. One of the site's very young members had already developed relations with a "little husband" and eventually wanted to marry him. Another female member had about ten "younger brothers" and two "elder sisters." The site seemed to have inspired her need for love or friendship through an adaptation of traditional family roles such as LG, LP, GG, JJ, etc. (老公 lao gong, 老婆 lao po, 哥哥 ge ge, 姐姐, jie jie). Several months into the social fashion of online marriage, Nongfu Mountain decided to institutionalize online divorce, as certain members were getting disappointed and wanted to break off their marriages.

When interviewing married fans, it became clear that they had taken their relationships quite seriously and were upset when they turned sour. Most interviewees admitted that their online affections were also seeping into the physical realm, as they had gone on to meet/hook up with their friends, or had started an actual relationship with their virtual husbands or wives.

The existence of these virtual family relations is also part of a gift economy driven by the process of sharing goods. For instance, researcher Lori Landay describes her process of finding "homes" on the virtual reality site Second Life, as friendships are created around acts of sharing objects and items in order to build homes:

Now I realize that part of the virtual economy is the gift economy, the exchange of items that can be transferred, and how exchanging, giving, and sharing objects can be part of friendships. In addition, virtual objects are not only meaningful for how they express identity, create environment, are aesthetically pleasing, or perform a compensatory function for unsatisfied desires in the actual world, but they can become significant because of their provenance, where they came from, who gave them to you. (Landay 2010)

Another example of virtual love based on a globalized gift economy can be seen in Lolita impersonators. These nostalgic-decadent girls can be seen as stick figures of the Japanese imagination, as they have conquered the hearts of young fans across cultures. Transnational media and fashion industries distribute Gothic Lolita products, which are then adapted by local consumers who act out the Lolita character. Their imagined relationships are indeed nurtured by a shared passion for the standardized products of "transnational bricolage," as Vera Mackie has named it:

> In economic terms, this generic profusion is expressed through multiple commodification. The commodities include clothing, accessories, publications, multimedia products and services. A host of industries has developed in order to produce, distribute, market and comment on these products and services. There are also shadow economies where second-hand products are swapped, bought and sold, or auctioned on e-bay style websites. The desires of the members of such subcultures as the Gothic Lolita fashion style can thus ultimately be linked to economic processes on a local, national, regional and global scale. (Mackie 2009)

Lolita love is characterized by a type of uneven relationship between an older male (Weird uncle (大叔) (怪叔叔/怪蜀黍) and younger female (Lolita 洛莉塔/萝莉), or vice versa, between an older female (禦姐) and a cute young boy (正太). In these relationships, Lolita herself is the key figure who acts out an exaggerated mode of innocence while showing an excessive desire for her older lover.[2] Most Lolita discussions and transactions take place online at blogging sites such as http://www.lolionline.net, where members look at each other's photo albums and share fashion tips. As Lolita Cynthia explained to me in an interview, this form of online self-portraiture is undertaken in order to experience an identity transformation: "It makes me more comfortable and makes me want to be in front of the camera more. It is more like a little mask that you wear in front of people. For instance, I smile a lot more when I am in my character. And then this becomes how people interpret me." Cynthia explains that her smile is not a faked one but is, rather, part of an active and ongoing construction of virtual love as a release from the everyday pressures of school, work, and family.

Except for their trendy platform shoes, Lolitas look like Victorian porcelain dolls (維多利亞式的瓷娃娃) who are wearing the clothes of bygone eras. In Hong Kong and mainland China they are often classified into three "types" – Classic Lolita who wears a simple white dress outfit, Sweet Lolita who dresses like a doll and in pink style, and Gothic Lolita who wears a black lacey dress and heavy gothic-style make-up. They inhabit a world of pre-sexual adolescence, their innocence emphasized through the heavy layering of vintage clothing and props. City gatherings are staged such as high tea parties where Lolitas eat sandwiches using forks and knives and pose for curious photographers and journalists.

Figure 3: Lolita impersonators in nostalgic lacey outfits at High Tea Party and Hong Kong Convention and Exhibition Center, April 2005.

They are exhibitionistic and media-savvy, but they also act decorously; their aesthetic of nostalgic decadence refers to older feudal bedrooms or secluded rose gardens where sexual seductions unfold slowly and with a sense of grace. Modes of well-mannered femininity are taken to an extreme in order to develop performative subjectivities. It suggests a play of dogmatic clichés as a means to construct libidinal agency within dominant discourses.

When Lolitas dress up and gather in public settings, they express a nostalgic kind of girlishness to embellish a city dominated by endless shopping malls and anonymous high-rise architecture. They can be seen as figures of high consumerism or male sexual fantasy, though they reclaim those stereotypes nostalgically by making their own outfits, dressing up together and preparing social outings in public spaces.

One aspect of the fantasy is the relationship of bondage between the young Lolita and her "weird uncles" (大叔) (怪蜀黍/怪叔叔), who are further classified into different types of respectable or grotesque older males, such as teachers (調教系), fashionable men (服裝系), or monsters and beasts (鬼畜系). Lolita is deeply in love with him but also has a broken heart, which signifies any number of difficulties or cultural prohibitions. These can be seen in a fan animation video and song posted on Youku.com.[3] Lolita is living in a beautiful old castle but she is actually chained by the ankle. In a flashback scene, she is seen walking around with a teddy bear and dancing her first steps of ballet. At the end of the story, her chain is broken by her older lover who has died in war. The lyrics of the song express her state of melancholy as it is simply too painful to "throw away her red shoes now."

或許從沒有愛上他
Maybe what I feel for is not him

隻是愛了童話
But a fairytale

那個野菊花開滿的窗台
A Wild chrysanthemums spreading its petals on the windowsill

窗帘卷起我的發
And curtains curling up my hair

我把紅舞鞋輕輕的丟下

The song then continues to praise a preserved state of innocence and youth:

你的白紙我來信手涂鴉
I left my graffiti on your white paper

沒有什麼比青春偉大
Nothing can beat my blooming youth

今天王子明天變成青蛙
Today's prince may become tomorrow's frog

By acting out a narcissistic girl who wants to bypass normal growth and jump into the adulthood of a romantic relationship, Lolita becomes part of a trend towards fantasy subjectivity and sexuality that needs to be protected and defined as such.

One way of intensifying the need for love and transgression is by becoming queer within the boundaries of animation culture. Within the freewheeling imagination of mainstream Japanese animation there are undercurrents of "slash fiction" practices where fans rewrite original stories and invent same-sex relationships between originally-straight characters. A related trend is for fans to embody and act out characters of the opposite gender and make appearances as cross-dressers. For instance, there is group of animation fans who consistently experiment with cross-dressing, posing in outfits of the opposite sex and posting photographs from their public appearances on online forums such as http://www.crossplay.net. Crossplay.net is an English-language site that allows costume players from various cultural backgrounds to chat, post blogs and upload photography albums. It offers practical support through chat rooms about costume critique, make-up tips and prop help, while also motivating them to discuss aspects of male-to-female or female-to-male transgender identity.

Male-to-female cross-dressers upload images of themselves in idealized girlish outfits and poses. The Hong Kong Cosplayer, Maggie Leung, uses a blog to share photographs of himself as Mikiyo Tsuda's character *Princess Prince*ss. (變身公主) This character appears in a series of stories about the forced feminization of school boys, who enter a high-class boarding school and are coached by seniors in order to become a princess and parade in front of the entire school. After becoming a princess, they are allowed to join a prestigious fraternity organization. Cross-dressing here is associated with traditional male anxiety and loyalty, but the story is also a queer underground comic that taps into the Japanese fascination with stifling high schools as seedbeds of perversion. It is a typical "frat boy" tale where feminization is associated with rituals of humiliation and male bonding, but it is also a queer story in its detailed obsession with the act of transitioning.

The rapid growth of Internet culture and Japan-inspired youth fads has produced a "prairie fire" of sexualized identities and queer stories. These animation genres are crucial in providing a creative outlet for youth. They also cause stark homophobic reactions in the mass media that are often replicated amongst fan groups themselves. Mark McLelland has documented how the eroticized depictions of underage characters and homosexual relationships in *yaoi* (矢追) or Boy Love (耽美) have outraged the mass media and influenced legislation in countries as diverse as Japan, Australia, Germany and China (McLelland 2000, 2009). But many of these stories and depictions are concocted by young female fans who do not have any sexually exploitative intentions.

Figure 4: Digital artwork of chained Lolita figure by Nori Tomizaki, From *Gothic Punk Lolita*.

for decades Japanese women and girls have imagined
love stories between beautiful boys
幾十年前，日本女子和女孩已開始幻想著美型男之間的愛情故事

Figure 5: Still from the shortfilm by Katrien Jacobs, *On the Japanese Doll Complex*, featuring Boy Love fan movie.

Nation-state governments and religious groups in diverse nation states are apt to ban the animation genre of Boy Love, and/or their attendant virtual communities, even though they are mostly benign and soft-core home-erotic fantasies. Rather than approaching young adults in an attempt to understand and interact with their queer fantasies and desires, the entire genre itself is banned in China because of it homosexual and "vulgar" content. In Hong Kong, the influx of Boy Love animation is at least several decades old, yet local media outlets and government policies have often fostered repressive attitudes and top-down policies. Mainland Chinese media were originally curious and supportive of the BL fad, but they began to shift their focus to BL's supposedly evil impact on youth as the subculture became popular and more visible (Liu 2009). For instance, one Chinese reporter claimed that Japanese comics were a cultural invasion and a threat to Chinese youth:

The popularity of these pornographic pocket comics will interrupt their academic study, distract these innocent kids, lower their moral standards, and weaken their legal sense ... Comic books peppered with heavy Japanese flavors, values and concepts will bring more damage to students. It is 'cultural hegemony' endangering Chinese kids. (Liu: 2009, Quote from Jingpao, 2001)

The female fans of BL comic books and movies are mostly interested in passionate homo-erotic love stories as a way to accumulate knowledge about queer sex or sex in general. Akikio Mizoguchi describes the mutual support between female readers as one of virtual lesbianism. The women bond deeply over their shared passions, in which their desire is also nurtured by a love for a specific type of male anatomy and male-male sex couplings, such as the dynamic between a "top" (在上者/施予者) and "bottom" (在下者/接受者), or "active" (主動) and "passive" (被動) partners. In this way, they can be thought of females with their own unique homosexual values. Indeed their virtual eroticism and sense of social community is somewhat determined by the fact that they are a distinctive and besieged minority group (Mizoguchi 2010).

In Hong Kong, several Boy Love comics were banned during the 2008 book fair after they had received complaints from customers concerning their sexually explicit imagery. Local newspapers such as *Ming Pao Daily* (明報) picked up on the ban but made very little effort to get a basic understanding of the animation culture (Ming Pao 2008). Blogger Min complained about *Ming Pao's* slanderous coverage of a "rotten girl family" in Hong Kong and Guanzhou. In the *Ming Pao* article, a local psychologist suggests that girls should be careful not to grow up with such novels, as they are sign of abnormal psychology. The article further stereotypes the BL fans or "addicts" as follows:

> They do not like shopping or dressing up, have little contact with outsiders, like to be at home playing games and watching anime movies, especially obsessed with "Boy Love" novels and comic books from Japan. They call themselves the "rotten girl" family. (*Ming Pao* 2008)

But indeed these rotten-girl families can be a powerful force in deconstructing persistent fears and anxieties about sexuality. Most BL fans in China and Hong Kong are happy to adopt the identity of a "rotten girl," based on the Japanese label of *fujoshi* (腐女). They are somewhat proud to be different and a member of a "rotten family." They are indeed nerdy girls or geek girls with a "bad girl" flavor. Like their male counter-partners, *otakus* (禦宅族/宅男), they are devoted to ACG anime products and their daily online routines. Fujoshi's also contributes to citizens' network culture and gift economies, as they utilize social networks in a search for new products offered and exchanged by the online community. Acts of sharing products and redrawing original content are encouraged, and members receive awards for carrying out "social services."

In some cases, BL fans will take a more activist approach and stand up for their rights of self-expression and sub-cultural status. In Shanghai in 2007 a group of fans protested against one of the Internet crackdowns on pornography, during which one of their favorite websites had been banned. They showed up at one of the government-sponsored Animation Tongren conventions (同人動畫) and inscribed satirical slogans on the convention's "scribble wall". As Tina Liu explains:

> After the state launched an anti-pornography campaign in April, 2007, *danmei* (BL) (耽美) participants turned the scribble wall at the East-Asian Comic and Animation *Tongren* Convention (東亞動漫同人大會) in Shanghai into a huge *fuqiang* (腐牆) in May 2007.

Figure 6: On the second day of the convention *danmei* participants turned the "scribble wall" into a "rotten wall." (Source no longer available).

Participants left messages such as "The party says we should build a road of *tongren* with Chinese characters, whereby BL is the predominant, with GL as a supplement," "The single spark of BL can start a prairie fire!" and "One who does not have *danmei* characteristics is not a person! One who does not have SM characters is not a good person!" (Liu 2008)

BL fans invented these satirical slogans to counteract the compulsively-moralistic government propaganda concerning "the harmonious family" and its concurrent need to repress deviance and uphold virtue. The differing strategies at least indicate the relative degrees of playfulness within each of the opposed camps.

This example of "the rotten girl family" shows that the adoption of virtual kinships have given many Chinese youth the opportunity to develop alternative life-styles. These queer fashions have become important instigators for reimagining the traditional nuclear family and its power and gender dynamics. Moreover, they also enable participants to transgress local prohibitions by fostering connections with transnational cultures and commodities.

Visual Ethnography: Documenting Backstage Gatherings and Rotating Personalities

When carrying out my observations of animation fans and Lolita impersonators over a 3-year period, I met with them several times and tried to gain an in-depth understanding of their social networks and their transition from everyday to fantasy guises. Since they waver between physical selves and the virtual worlds of animation, I tried to gain insight into how they layer their various personalities. Moreover, being sensitive to the fact that they often wished to hide their private affairs and sexual identities, the Cosplay zone was examined as a space for temporary or tentative explorations of subjectivity. The aim was to follow moments of transitioning between different personalities. Their remarkable public appearances were ephemeral and to some extent "unreal," or conditioned by fictional narratives and fantasy worlds.

Costume players tend to show off their wavering or rotating personalities while they protect and hide their "authentic" physical selves and relationships. This means that research must also examine how and why they hide and reveal complex subjectivities. For instance, a group of *Kigurumi* costume (布偶装) players in Taipei decided, when visited, not to be filmed or photographed as their actual physical selves. They were mostly biological straight males who wanted to cross-dress and make appearances as "pretty girls," wearing the costumes of female animation figures complete with a doll-like mask. King Fabulous was the artist who crafted their extraordinary masks and who encouraged them to dress up in a specific fashion and then make public appearances. These costume players, constituting a kind of a family, organized a dressing up session and then allowed me only to document and take extensive photographs and video footage of their Cosplay parade.

Figure 7: Online photographs of Kigurumi Cosplayers and cross-dressers from Taiwan. Avalailable at http://sharkgogo.myweb.hinet.net.

The Kigurumi Cosplayers probably wanted to hide their everyday male identities to protect themselves from social stigmatization. Nevertheless, I was able to spend time with them and observe how they rotate or transition between male and female selves. In order to fully grasp their social psychology, I spent time with them in various stages of costuming and therefore witnessed their ongoing appearances. In other words, I tried to somehow melt into their lengthy session of dressing up and self- photography. I also tried on one of their restrictive body suits, which they typically wear underneath these girlish outfits. They definitely opened up after they noticed that I also like to dress up on occasion. I thus explored a unique type of immersion with them, while sharing my research and asking whether their appearances could be further explored or documented. By asking them to what extent they wanted to collaborate and be filmed, I became more aware of the pleasures and emotional complexities involved in transitioning.

At sanctified public spaces such as the Hong Kong Convention and Exhibition center (香港會展中心), Costume players tend to gather in corridors next to the main exhibition hall, or they are assigned a special room where they are free to hang out and parade their latest fashions (自製服裝). In any case, only a small percentage of them would actually be making any official appearances within competitions or the ACG convention. They transition in the "backstage room," where they spend several hours parading and taking photos. The

Figure 8: Cosplayers at the ACG conventions at the Hong Kong Convention and Exhibition Center, August 2007. Photos by Robert Iolini.

backstage room is a cozy, messy space, allowing fans to gather in small groups, as they apply make-up, dress and generally get ready to appear as a character.

The backstage room is different from the competition space but it is a still a heavily-mediated space, as it exemplifies the new era of digital photography and social networking. Most Cosplayers engage in fervent self-photography or photographic collaboration with designated peer photographers. They develop relationships with these photographers, who act as loyal pals whose role is to capture their newest outfits and poses. In short, it is an amateur performative space where posers/players and watchers/photographers symbiotically coexist in order to fondly admire a specific type of variety show.

In my efforts to capture these variety shows, I have drawn on the field of visual anthropology. For several decades scholars in anthropology have analyzed the power structures inherent in acts of producing ethnographic accounts and audio-visual documentation. The Visual Anthropology Journal was launched in the early 1990s as an interdisciplinary effort to develop discourses around the collaboration between scholars and communities. Renowned scholars such as Lucien Taylor and Victor Burgin, and filmmakers such as Trinh T. Minh-ha, participated in extensive dialogues concerning the artistic and responsible modes of documenting various cultures.

Since costume play is a predominantly visual or pictorial medium where players intensely bond with each other through DIY photography, I observed their photography sessions and also took part in them. It was clear from the outset that costume players like to pose for photography, while being generally reticent or resistant to being interviewed and articulating their hobbies. Posing and DIY photography were a more natural way for them to communicate their talent and social bonds. Even though I did not belong to their peer group, they also were happy to pose and make appearances for the odd viewer. Secondly, the project became a study of (in)visibility as I entered into more complex relationships with a small number of Cosplayers and negotiated how they wanted to be filmed and how they might be able to give more in-depth interviews. During these interviews I tried to ask questions about their everyday lives and relationships, but it was always difficult or nearly impossible to probe more sensitive issues around their sexuality.

From the initial photo sessions, introductory meetings and onwards, I carried out three phases of observation and interviews over a time-span of three years (June 2007–June 2010). I visited about ten ACG/Cosplay conventions in Hong Kong that typically took place at the Hong Kong Convention Center, and at various universities. I also made field trips to Tokyo and Beijing. At the same time, I observed Cosplay participants on social networking websites such as deviantart.com and cure.com, where Cosplayers develop their profiles and socialize with each other. All in all, I conducted short interviews with about twenty Cosplayers, alone or with friends at these various locations, and took many photographs, along with making extensive video recordings. Since the atmosphere during those gatherings is very noisy and hectic and since Cosplayers are busy with their social activities, I then tried to convince some of them to meet later for in-depth interviews.

Queer (Dis)appearances – Kin and Maggie/Martin

I made deeper case studies about two experienced Cosplayers in Hong Kong, conducting several in-depth interviews with them about the social psychology of costume play and its relation to sexual identity. We invited Cosplayers Kin and Maggie to dress up in a TV studio so that we could witness their process of identity transformation, while taking photographs and video footage in order to capture the moment of transitioning. Even though it was hard for us to enter into deep conversations with them, we tried to catch them in the heat of the moment. Both Cosplayers have had several years of experience as cross-dressers, but their stories and life-styles stand for a different type of attachment. Kin's appearances are typical of the Cosplay scene in that they are casual and ephemeral. She likes to dress like a male and she shows a high tolerance for queers, but she does not want to reveal or share information about her sexual relationships. She will not allow outsiders to know to what extent her identity is queer.

Maggie on the other hand is an openly-queer cross-dresser and transgendered person. She was very happy to be involved in this study and eventually also shared information about her transsexual friends and families. Maggie wants to belong to both Cosplay and transgendered groups. She is not judgmental about different types of transgendered identity. In this way she also asserts her own kind of open or flexible identity as an essential freedom or deviation from the norm.

Kin is a female Cosplayer and cross-dresser who largely takes on male identities in her role-play. She is a well practiced expert in producing and validating Cosplay knowledge and she also questions the worn-out dynamic between female models and male photographers. She herself works with a circle of female friends who act as both models and photographers at Cosplay events. In most cases, the cultivation of rotating selves take place within a larger group of people and online communities, while more authentic bonds are only developed in smaller circles that mostly remain hidden to outsiders. When interviewing Kin, she told us that she had impersonated more than a hundred characters over a span of ten years. She tried on different outfits and make-up styles in a fluctuating idea of masculinity that she also engaged with psychologically. She started out impersonating J-rock celebrities and then moved on to *yaoi* characters (耽美角色) and Japanese warriors from animation stories. One of her outfits is that of the character Senguku from the animation story *Date Masamune* (伊達正宗). He is a warrior from ancient times wearing six giant swords and dressed in a fierce rubber outfit. He is also wears an eye-patch as he was known to be blind in one eye after having consumed his own eyeball.

When asked to reflect on her life and growth as a cross-player, Kin explains that she eventually got better at it and now knows how to do it a in a more energetic way. She also believes that she may grow out of the habit, as her parents have put pressure on her to quit. One time I ran into Kin at one of the conventions at Hong Kong Polytechnic University. She was wearing a long blue gown and was surrounded by a group of male photographers. It was the first time that she had attracted so many male photographers but they had mistaken her for a female character. She was actually embodying a male character who is known for wearing a feminine type of gown. Usually she only poses for her own small group of women photographer friends. As she explains:

> I was pretty shocked about that as for the last ten years I have seldom been surrounded by male photographers. I am not used to them as I usually work with female photographers. We create our own events and take photographers along, sometimes in private home spaces, and sometimes in public parks.

In regard to public reactions to her male personas, she answers that she knows that men in Hong Kong and Taiwan are dismissive of these types of characters. She does see it is as female rebellion, as an honest expression of "tough femininity," as "women in Hong Kong can actuality can be very strong and convey a sense of independence." As for sexual orientation, she is unwilling to speak about her love life. She explains that she is very supportive of queer relationships and this is what makes her different from other Cosplayers. We never got to meet any of Kin's Cosplay or queer friends but she admitted that she had engaged in this peculiar life-style for ten years and it would be difficult to cast off when she eventually matured out of her Cosplay phase. Kin disappeared from my project after several interviews without explanation. She had expressed several times during interviews that she was ready to "retire from Cosplay" and that her mother was putting her under a lot of pressure to do so. It became clear to me that she was perhaps unwilling to share further personal details and that she was transitioning back into a "responsible" heterosexual adulthood.

Maggie is a MTF cross-dresser and Cosplayer (男扮女裝角色扮演愛好者) who uses female costumes to explore a more deeply-felt transgendered identity, which she is also in the process of adopting in actual life. In this way, Maggie differs from cross-players like Kin who like to wear costumes of the opposite gender, but do not wish to openly pursue a queer identity. When I first met Maggie Leung she was dressed up in a school uniform and had a tomboy-like appearance. She explained that she was the female tomboy character Mizuki from the manga story *Hanakimi* (花样少男少女). Mizuki wants to cross-dress like a school boy in order to enter the school of a boy whom she has a deep crush on. Maggie used the character of Mizuki to express her own uniquely fluctuating and queer identity. In a second interview, conducted at the City University of Hong Kong, Maggie was dressed as the character Ai Enma (閻魔愛)from the cartoon *Hell Girl* (地獄少女). Ai Enma is a supernatural force who can be contacted by those whose hearts are burning with hatred and then she will help them enact revenge. Maggie was impersonating this spirit, wearing a Japanese female kimono. She was carrying a curse doll and stretching out its right arm, just as Hell Girl would have performed in a movie.

Figure 9: The Rotating Personalities of Hong Kong Cosplayer and cross-dresser Maggie Leung – Gothic Lolita and Hell Girl. Photos by Andrew Guthrie.

Maggie was interviewed a third time in the TV Studio of the City University of Hong Kong's Department of Media and Communication (香港城市大學媒體與傳播系). This studio is a large comfortable space with a room for people to get dressed in and put on their make-up. We made sure that no other people would be around during the time of the interview and gave Maggie a chance to dress up in an outfit of her choice. She chose the outfit of Gothic Lolita and was wearing a back lacey dress, black gloves and a little back bonnet on the head. She explained later that she had chosen this outfit because it was a fashion-style for her rather than an outfit associated with a specific cartoon character.

When she cross-dresses as Gothic Lolita, she taps into a different type of subculture and goes out with other, biological, women who are interested in their own Lolita impersonations. She thus gets a chance to be surrounded by other women who adopt and manipulate their nostalgic and decadent girlish outfits. In order to clarify her interest in the Lolita figure, she shows several photographs of herself at public outings surrounded by a group of women. She is mostly well accepted by these women as a transgendered person and indeed some of them have become personal friends.

She was happy to share several stages of the transformation process, starting in the dressing room when she was putting on make-up where she explained the various details of her cross-dressing routine as Gothic Lolita. During this extensive session it became clear

Figure 10: Cross-dresser Maggie Leung (lower left) on a public outing with other, female, Lolita impersonators.

that she manifests a transgendered identity by using costume play gatherings as one of the venues for identity exploration. She explained that there was a community of cross-players who worked like this, but they wished to remain hidden and were not willing to talk to researchers.

When asked if other costume players are aware of her transgendered identity, she answered that they do not really care about that as they are just focused on embodying certain characters. She added that she herself was not sure if she was a cross-dresser (異裝愛好者) or a transsexual (跨性別人士). She was taking hormones and contemplating sexual reassignment surgery, but not sure if she could afford it and if s/he would get any support from family members. In traditional notions of the Chinese family one is required to live with your biological parents and with "what your parents have given you." It had become, for Maggie, an "exhausting inner struggle" to try to live like that. Maggie's parents are aware of the situation and know that she is consulting with a therapist to prepare for sexual realignment surgery, but overall they do not support Maggie's wishes. She also explained that she does not trust the medical system in Hong Kong, as they do not seem to be fully engaged in the medical and social aspects of her case. As a matter of fact, several months later Maggie told us that her application for sexual reassignment surgery had been abandoned as the specific unit she was working with had lost its funding.

When I asked Maggie about her sexual orientation, she explained that she would be interested in meeting lesbian women or "TBs" tomboys (女同志中扮演男性角色的一方). A "TB" or Tomboy in the Hong Kong context is a young masculine-looking woman who also develops lesbian relationships. The TB and her partner TBG (Tomboy Girl) roles are specifically associated with all-girl high schools. Maggie emphasized several times that the biological gender of her partner was not important. We thus found out that Maggie would take on female characters within Costume Play, the Gothic Lolita subculture and cross-dressing communities to bond with like-minded transgenders. She was still devoted to the biological family and lived with them, but spent most of her free time meeting with people who could share her queer hobbies and life-styles.

We had two additional meetings with Maggie which made us understand the social support systems available to her.

Figure 11: Researchers on a daytrip with Maggie Leung. We followed Maggie from her home in Shatin to a hidden place in Tsuen Wan where s/he likes to dress up in a small rented apartment.

UNIVERSITY OF WINCHESTER
LIBRARY

Figure 12: Hong Kong Transsexuals Omena and Joanna at a research gathering to discuss transgendered identity.

Figure 13: Hong Kong Transsexual Natalie browsing the Facebook group for women and "Fake Girls" Girlz Kingdom.

Figure 14: Screenshot of the Facebook Group for Women and Fake Girls *Girlz Kingdom*.

In one meeting we accompanied Maggie from her home space in Shatin to a space in Tsuen Wan, where she rented a small room in order to get dressed-up on a regular basis. She liked to go to this tiny room to get changed and create some distance from the living environment of the biological family. The rent of this room was quite affordable and shared amongst a group of cross-dressers who are all more or less in the same situation – they needed a cheap and safe place to put on their feminine clothes. Sometimes they would hang out and dress together and keep each other informed about cross-dressing fashions and outfits.

Several months after openly discussing transgendered social life-styles, Maggie contacted us again and told us that she wanted to introduce us to other transgendered and transsexual friends. We met on a Sunday afternoon in a private home with a group of four transsexuals – Rob, Natalie, Omena, and Joanne. We conducted short interviews with all of them about their use of social networks and support groups and their use as alternative "families." Joanne was the oldest transsexual who viewed herself as Maggie's "mother." Joanne helped Maggie through various stages of her complicated life. Maggie confirmed that Joanna was her mother and that she got along with her very well as she could easily read her mind.

Omena was a younger transsexual who was friends with Maggie. She was generally wary of cross-dressers who only dress up for fetishistic purposes, but she believed that Maggie was different and more of a transsexual. She had had several sexual reassignment surgeries and belonged to a virtual community of about 10,000 people who helped her go through the surgeries and post-surgery process. She joined this community by posting pictures of herself and she received many critical responses about how to improve her feminine looks. She was generally very happy to receive this kind of feedback and also became somewhat of an Internet celebrity by gradually documenting her new looks. She was fully transitioned and wanted to be addressed as a female, but was also happy to explain her transformation process to researchers.

Lastly, we interviewed a young cross-dresser Natalie who was only 20 years old and not sure how to develop a transgendered identity. Natalie was hooked on a virtual group on Facebook called Girlz Kingdom, which is a forum and photography archive for biological women, cross-dressers and transsexuals who were all pursuing the look of a "fake girl." Many members posted pictures of themselves as "fake girls," aspiring to be cute-looking girl with immaculate feminine features.

By interviewing Maggie's transsexual family, we understood that they all have different ways of conceiving of the relationship between popular culture and sexuality. Some members of the family were tolerant of Cosplay mobs and youngsters trying out cross-dressing styles, while others were dismissive of these more shallow and temporary habits. Natalie and Maggie, being the younger transsexuals in this group, were more inspired by visual fantasy cultures. Joanna and Omena had gone through sexual reassignment surgery and to some extent wanted to deny or halt the existence of transgenderism as rotating selves.

The Closet With Revolving Door

Animation fandom is a peculiar way for Chinese youth to explore aspects of queer sexuality, which they may or may not adopt, as embodied subjectivities and life-styles. Japanese characters allow Chinese people to assume tentative or temporary sexual identities. The Japanese ACG industries have responded well to a need for soft-core homo-erotic or transgendered content, but these industries are profit-driven engines of change and have little interest in developing a more confident queer media culture.

Rather than suggesting that these animation fan groups will eventually contribute to queer identity politics, we have to consider the fact that they are culturally restrained and different from non-Chinese queer groups. When interviewing Rob, a FTM transsexual who moves and lives between Hong Kong and London, he explained that it was easier for him to be member of a "queer family" in London. He would meet with them on a regular basis and had developed bonds with them in ways that were beyond regular friendships. He believed that UK society shows more support towards transgendered individuals, even though there is, on average, more random violence directed at transgendered or gay people in Britain. He explains that each of these cultures have different ways of accommodating transsexuality. He is ultimately optimistic about his move back to Hong Kong and improving relations with his biological family.

One way of understanding people's need to disengage from identity politics is by considering the cultural passages and prohibitions of transitioning and role-play. Terre

Thaemlitz has defined the cross-dressing individual as a person who may live in a "closet with a revolving door." Some queers or transgender people argue for identity groups based on their acceptance of alternative bodies and politics, while others may still wish to endlessly diverge from these proposals or simply remain invisible. The power of queerness may be exactly located in its tentative or open-ended status or lack of homogeneous materialization and visibility. Thaemlitz makes an argument against the politics of representation for MTF transgender (男扮女裝/男變女) people and shows that many are actually living as in-between subjectivities. He criticizes MTF people (男扮女裝的人/男變女者) who are too obsessed with a solid idea of femininity or with the desire of trying to pass:

> For myself, the power of trans-genderism – if any – rests in this vagueness and divisiveness. It is not a power of distinction or difference from other genders, but rather the power of seeing representational systems of distinction or difference between genders collapse. It is not a power of transformation, but rather the power of transition. It is not a "third gender" offering unity, or a middling of genders. It is, by all means, a threat to the myth of social unity. Within the transgendered community, it is the potential to de-essentialise acts of transitioning in relation to social process. (Thaemlitz 2008)

Other scholars have stressed the importance of processual sexuality and fictionalization as a mechanism of the self and its social cohesion. For instance, African-American gay youth of the ballroom scene dress up and transition together, while also becoming part of queer families or "houses" (Arnold and Bailey 2009). As seen in Jennie Livingston's well-known documentary movie, *Paris is Burning* (1991), gay men become highly-flamboyant characters in ballroom performances while they are often experiencing dire material circumstances in their everyday lives. The imagined family structure helps this group to stay afloat as marginalized subjects, while support is expressed through collaborations in making outfits and organizing performances in the ballroom. Arnold and Bailey have closely observed one of these families, called the House of Prestige, where they analyzed its non-heteronormative kinship structures or "kinscripts." One of the remarkable features of the ballroom community is that it has developed its own gender-sex system, where family members have a queer mother, a practical nurturer who tries to be constantly available for them, and a queer father who gives more abstract advice about life-style choices and ethical dilemmas. The family members learn to adopt a variety of gender roles, including butch queen, femme queen, butch queen up in drags, butch, man and woman. When interviewing members of the ballroom community, cross-dressers explain that their identities are "more theatrics than family bonds" but that they also, through these interactions, have started to care for each other on a deeper level. Their fictitious transformations into upper-class celebrities or fashion supermodels help them recast and share their social lives and individual concerns.

Chinese Cosplayers live in very different kind of queer ballroom, as they mostly do not live out their inclinations nor reveal themselves as sexual minorities. However, they are happy to be social outcasts and form intense bonds with other like-minded individuals.

They develop their own kind of "kinscripts" or structures based on fantasy characters and acts of cross-dressing. One group of costume players in Beijing and Shanghai openly calls itself the NKNL family. Atom is one of the members of this impromptu family and explains that it encompasses two types of relationships. First of all it refers to a grouping of like-minded costume players who gather and travel to remote places to make "visual art" and develop rotating personalities. As she explains:

> I want to say something about my Cosplay family. We come from a league named "NKNL" (no kuso no life … no passion no life), built over four years, with mainly members from Beijing and Shanghai. We share a belief that Cosplay can be a kind of visual art instead of just expressing the willingness to emulate a fondness of characters. We try to make Cosplay photos that represent scenes and presences in original works. Sometimes we travel to a remote and concealed place to find appropriate camera scenes. After the acts of photography we create a series of photos with a text telling a story, and we insert coordinated music to create atmosphere. Maybe it sounds like some multimedia acts but we'd like to call this a kind of "paper-movie."

The second type of relationship in Atom's family exists between a smaller group of people within the NKNL family who provide deeper levels of support, friendship and love. Atom has developed a close friendship with Franseca, who is a talented artist and the designated Cosplay photographer of the family. Both Atom and Franseca like to Cosplay together and take on masculine roles. They also believe that they physically resemble each other's androgynous female type. When interviewing Franseca, she explains that she cannot distinguish her love and desire for her family members from her love for their characters. She does not see this as a problem but as a specific relationship that she wants to foster. She is very tolerant towards queers in general and believes that the Cosplay community in Beijing has overall generated positive support for queers.

In "Otaku Sexuality" Tamaki Saito explains that the sexuality of animation fans is driven their attachment to ongoing fictionality. (Saito 2007: 237) Tamaki defends *otaku* sexuality as a specific type of experience that allows subjects to be confused and waver between actuality and fictions. Precisely by entering a radical sexual confusion, young people are encouraged to immerse themselves in, conquer and possess other worlds.

In contrast to a defense of radical confusion, queer scholars have pointed out that popular culture fan groups are often dismissive of actual queer bodies and minority groups. Rosi Braidotti has critiqued the popularization and dissolution of queerness in the European political context. She believes that neo-liberal politicians imagined fantastic possibilities for feminism and multiculturalism, but their rhetoric was deliberately divorced from historical developments and a sincere desire for social change. These propositions were trendy and opportunistic, carrying the seeds of their own depletion along with a denial of actual marginal subjects. Her critique of queer pop culture is also directed at neo-liberalism as a rushed commercialization of previously-marginalized communities. As she writes:

Advanced capitalism is a difference engine – a multiplier of de-territorialised differences, which are packaged and marketed under the labels of 'new, hybrid and multiple or multicultural identities'. It is important to explore how this logic triggers a vampiric consumption of 'others', in contemporary social and cultural practice. From fusion-cooking to 'world music', the consumption of 'differences' is a dominant cultural practice. Jackie Stacey, in her analysis of the new organic food industry argues that we literally eat the global economy. Paul Gilroy reminds us that we also wear it, listen to it and watch it on our many screens, on a daily basis. (Braidotti 2005: 2)

We could similarly ask the question – is animation fandom an easy and flighty substitute for actual queer tolerance and love? Do the elaborate role-playing efforts and dressing-up sessions of queer fans aim to materialize into lasting bonds or do they only mimic the possibilities of queerness?

The Cosplay zone allows fans to explore a smooth and ambiguous kind of nonconformity as they model themselves on the stars and starlets of animation culture. Fans follow certain edgy Japanese life-styles as an escape from the restrictions and stigmas within Chinese sex culture. The excessive knowledge and impersonation of these styles helps people generate fictions that suspend local social pressures and cultural constraints. Lisa Rofel has pointed out in *Desiring China: Experiments in Neoliberalism, Sexuality, and Public Culture* that sexual innovation is almost always expressed through a rhetoric of benign consumerist fashion and entertainment. People acknowledge their attachment to material lifestyles precisely to avoid or bypass the "dangerous passions of politics" (Rofel 2007: 121). That does not mean that Chinese animation fans are utterly materialistic but that they mask their non-traditional queer friendships by engaging in socially-acceptable commodity consumption.

As explained before, some female animation fans are intrigued by depictions of homosexual relations, yet they may not be interested in exploring gay or lesbian sexuality. As a matter of fact, when asked to comment on these issues, they are often dismissive of queer sexuality. Several Boy Love fans told me that they may read one or two Boy Love novels a week, but they would not be able to accept any real homosexual relationships or endorse gay rights. Their imagined gay relations are often divorced from references to actual gay sexuality. Kinsella explains this phenomenon in this way:

Although the characters of these stories are biologically male, in essence they are genderless ideal types, combining favoured masculine qualities with favoured feminine qualities ... Young female fans feel more able to imagine and depict idealized strong and free characters if they are male. (Kinsella 2000: 117)

Two female crossplayers, Huen and Yuko, emphatically explain that their love for queer characters says nothing about their sexual orientation. Huen is interested in history and often plays the Prussian King Frederic the Great, from *Hetalia : Axis Powers* (百無一用意呆利). This manga itself is famous as it personifies different, incongruous countries through a

Figure 15: Cosplayers Huen (upper left) and Yuko (lower right) surrounded by their peers at the Extra/Ordinary Dresscode Event, City University of Hong Kong and Videotage, November 2009.

variety of characters, combining all their histories into a single narrative. As Huen explains, she enjoys Cosplay because it is tolerant towards queer content yet she cannot find suitable boys to date in real life:

> I have thought about this a lot when I was studying for a BA degree in Cultural Studies. I think that Cosplay is the only legal way to let us experience a transgender identity and homosexuality and it accepts them tolerantly.

Yuko explains that this love for queer characters is not related to actual sexual orientation or sex, as they want to come across as "normal":

> Even though we are just ordinary people, we read BL and boys read GL and some boys pretend to be girls, but we are normal in sex orientation. But it is just that we may have a worse impression about actual males than ordinary people.

Huen compares this attitude to Hong Kong's "tomboy girls" who may act out a masculine identity and have same-sex relations in high school, but eventually may not want to become lesbians. When probed further about their sexual orientation, Huen and Yuko explain that they just like the male characters from BL and cannot love such men in real life. They are a bit frustrated in finding men whom they would really like to date and go out with, who are also fond of animation characters.

Conclusion

When talking about sexual uprisings in China, it is essential to take into account the influence of Japanese ACG culture. As explained in earlier chapters, China's cultural-erotic mindset is in constant dialogue with the products of Japanese sex entertainment. This includes genres of animation culture that have allowed for stories of queer love, transsexualism, and soft-core eroticism. Animation fans and Costume players are driven by "liminal" (or: half-materialized) eroticism or a sexuality of ongoing reinvention. As shown in the statements by female fans of gay love stories, they impersonate queer sexuality "to a certain extent" and also feel the need to disengage from it. They help each other in performing unusual characters but their hobby also becomes a displaced substitute for a longer-term commitment to queer lifestyles. Rather than wanting to belong to one subcultural or queer group, they develop rotating personalities and cross-dressing fashions to create an open space for artistic creativity and alliances.

The nagging question underlying my observations is whether these ongoing acts of transitioning and fictionalizing identity become part of their adult psychology and cultural lifestyles. Even though one can see that they are basically engaged in ephemeral youth fads, it also points to a desire for more profound cultural change and diversified sexual options.

When observing the virtual families of costume players, we found that many youths are eager to show off same-sex love, but we could only guess how these appearances might become more than a passing phase or fad. Most of our informants carefully obscured their actual relationships and disappeared at crucial moments within the process of interlocution and revelation. One reason why they do not wish to further pursue a queer sexual identity is that they are put under pressure by their families and cultural institutions to "break the habit" and grow up into responsible adults. Many of the people I have interviewed have spoken of unsupportive families and homophobic reactions, so it would be hard for them to carry the official LGBT label. In this respect, it was important to examine multiple personalities and their patterns of (dis)appearance as subjectivities that may never substantially hold together or fully materialize.

People use the Japanese animation culture to explore a fascination with queer genres and transgendered characters. Both female and males wish to adopt traits of innocent femininity proposed by Japanese animation and Gothic Lolita culture. These stock figures of transnational bricolage have given rise to boundless cults and interpretation in cities all over Asia, but they nevertheless are modeled on a narrow ideal of beauty. Rosi Braidotti is one scholar who is critical of the neo-liberal economic premise behind this ideal, seeing as it leaves behind the physicality and social conditions of actual minorities and their difficult processes of transitioning. Terre Thaemlitz has equally forwarded an eloquent critique of transgendered "glam" cultures arguing that they mimic the opulence-driven glamour of *haute couture* (Thaemlitz 2008). Similarly, we could ask if the performative Japanese subcultures are harsh on actual queers because they are less "cute" and have different standards of fashion and embodiment. Even though many Cosplayers know that they will never be able to become as beautiful as the model of their chosen animation characters, they hold onto this ideal as the most repeated line in their unwritten bible.

While virtual homes and families help Cosplayers to transition, they are indeed harsh on themselves and judgmental towards those who happen to diverge from the character's deeply-ingrained model cuteness. We were told many times during interviews that Cosplayers use anonymous online identities to write very negative critiques of each other's appearances and outfits. The Cosplay groups are based on elusive ideals of queerness that exists only in spurts and can only be captured and identified by very inquisitive, insistent and nosy outsiders.

Notes

1. The coded vocabulary for these family roles goes as follows: LG: Chinese Pinyin "laogong," means husband; LP: Chinese Pinyin "laopo," means wife; GG: Chinese Pinyin "gege," means elder brother; JJ: Chinese Pinyin "jiejie," means elder sister; DD: Chinese Pinyin "didi," means younger brother; MM: Chinese Pinyin "meimei," means younger sister.
2. The definitions of Lolita relationships were taken from the Chinese Interactive encyclopedia Baidu. http://baike.baidu.com/view/2864.html?tp=0_01 and http://baike.baidu.com/view/4575.html?tp=5_11 (accessed 11 July 2011) The source of weird uncle classifications is the sina blog

post by 喧嚣学院), "The most dangerous ten kinds of men for women" http://blog.sina.com.cn/s/blog_4ad1dc7e0100ay4o.html, 28 September, 2008, (accessed 11 July 2011).
3. The Lolita video and song was found on youku.com, http://v.youku.com/v_show/id_XMTA2MTY0ODc2.html (accessed 11 July 2011)

References

Arnold, Emily and Bailey, Marlon (2009) "Constructing Home and Family: How the Ballroom Community Supports African American GLBTQ Youth in the Face of HIV/ AIDS," *Journal of Gay & Lesbian Social Services*, 21: 2, pp. 171–88.

Braidotti, Rosi (2005) "A Critical Cartography of Feminist Post-Postmodernism," *Australian Feminist Studies*, 20: 47, pp.169–79.

Iwabuchi, Koichi (2002) *Recentering Globalization: Popular Culture and Japanese Transnationalism*, Durham: Duke University Press.

Jingbao (2001) "Porn invades students' pockets" Seqing duwu ruqin xuesheng koudai (色情读物 " 入侵" 学生口袋) in *Jingbao* (晶报), Shenzhensheqing (深圳社情), Shenzhen, 8 November.

Kinsella, Sharon (2000) *Adult Manga: Culture and Power in Contemporary Japanese Society,* Honolulu: ConsumAsiaN, Curzon Press and the University of Hawaii.

Landay, Lori (2010) "Rethinking Virtual Commodification, or The Virtual Kitchen Sink," *Virtual World Research*, 2: 4 (online) https: //journals.tdl.org/jvwr/article/view/860/625 (accessed 11 July 2011).

Liu, Tina (2009) "Conflicting Discourses on Boys' Love and Subcultural Tactics in Mainland China and Hong Kong," in Mark McLelland and Fran Martin (eds.) *Intersections: Gender and Sexuality in Asia and the Pacific* http://intersections.anu.edu.au/issue20/liu.htm (accessed 11 July 2011).

Livingston, Jennie (1991) *Paris is Burning.* (DVD) Off white, Miramax.

Mackie, Vera (2009) "Transnational Bricolage: Gothic Lolita and the Political Economy of Fashion," In Mark McLelland and Fran Martins (eds) *Intersections: Gender and Sexuality in Asia and the Pacific,* 20April http://intersections.anu.edu.au/issue20/mackie.htm (accessed 11 July 2011).

McLelland, Mark (2009) "(A)cute Confusion: The Unpredictable Journey of Japanese Popular Culture," in Mark McLelland and Fran Martin (eds) *Intersections: Gender and Sexuality in Asia and the Pacific,* 20 April, http://intersections.anu.edu.au/issue20/mclelland.htm (accessed 29 July 2011).

McLelland, Mark (2000) "No Climax, No Point, No Meaning? Japanese Women's Boy-Love Sites on the Internet," *Journal of Commercial Inquiry*, 24: 3, pp. 52–69.

Ming Pao (2007) "Hong Kong Book Fair to Sell Pornographic Comics," *Ming Pao Daily* (online) 24 July, (no longer available).

Mizoguchi, Akiko (2010) "Towards Activism of Pleasure: Possibilities of Yaoi as a Productive Queer Forum," paper delivered at the *ACS Crossroads* conference, Lingnan University, Hong Kong, June.

Orbaugh, Sharalyn (2003) "Busty Battlin' Babes: the Evolution of the Shojo in 1990s Visual Culture," Norman Bryson, Maribeth Graybill, and Joshua Mostow (eds) *Gender and Power in the Japanese Visual Field,* Honolulu: Hawaii University Press (pp. 200–28).

Rofel, Lisa (2007) *Desiring China: Experiments in Neoliberalism, Sexuality, and Public Culture,* Durham: Duke University Press.

Saito, Tamaki (2007) "Otaku Sexuality," in Christopher Bolton, Istvan Csicsery-Ronay jr. and Takyuki Tatsumi (eds) *Robot Ghosts and Wired Dreams. Japanese Science Fictions from Origins to Anime,* Minneapolis: University of Minnesota Press (pp. 222–50).

Thaemlitz, Terre (2008) "Viva McGlam: Is Transgenderism a Critique of or Capitulation to Opulence-Driven Glamour Models?" http://www.comatonse.com/writings/vivamcglam.html (accessed 10 July 2011).

Wong, Wendy Siuyi (2006) "Globalizing Manga: From Japan to Hong Kong and Beyond," in Lunning Frenchy (ed) *Mechademia 1: Emerging Worlds of Anime and Manga* (pp.23–45).

Conclusion

People's pornography refers to a sexual rebellion within China's netizen culture. The book unravels a Chinese quest for arousal and expressivity alongside several media industries – Chinese DIY videos, blogging domains, arthouse cinema, Japanese Adult Videos and Japanese animation. People's pornography is a way for people to reclaim access to sexually explicit media, and to create their own cultural heritage and local identities alongside a wealth of transnational products. In mainland China, there is an antithetical reaction of neo-liberal stimulus and despotic cruelty to this wealth. There are very few formal mechanisms, little democratic dialogue or enlightened education to sort out this confusion. In this regard, China differs from older and more established "porn empires" like the USA and Japan, whose governments have grappled more openly with their artists of the obscene imagination and their porn industries.

The book shows that Chinese netizens have taken it upon themselves to conduct dialogues and share erotic or pornographic materials. A recent peek at China's social network Weibo (微博), the equivalent of the banned network Twitter, shows that sex talk flourishes around digital celebrities such as Japanese porn star Sola Aoi and Chinese sex blogger Mu Zimei. As a matter of fact, Mu Zimei managed to make a full comeback in 2011 on Weibo after a first stab at Confucian morality in 2003. We can see that the netizen culture is thriving and throbbing, even if it is still very vulnerable, as many of the major players are prone to censorship or outright criminalization. Since I observed one of the fiercest bouts of government repression around Spring 2011, during the concluding phases of writing this book, it was difficult to round off my analysis with a bright prophecy for China's porn cultures. But I had enough evidence to foresee major changes in young people's attitude towards sex and sex talk.

Recent Chinese anti-obscenity campaigns reveal prejudice against low art or sex culture itself as it is being directed against the "three vulgarities" (三俗) – "vulgar," "kitschy" and "degraded" art (低俗、庸俗、媚俗). These three types of art, by directive, are to be avoided by Chinese people, but the terms are so vague and potentially all-encompassing that almost any contemporary artwork might be considered as such. These campaigns are utterly serious, even though the idea that any post-industrial nation state could halt this boom in art and pop culture appears to be preposterous. Under this campaign there is indeed a tendency to squash a sense of humor and criticism, as it was reported that there already have been public criticisms against popular comedians such as Zhou Libo (周立波) and Xiao Shenyang (小潘陽) (SCMP 2010). Another example is the April 2011 detainment of the Ai Wei Wei (艾未未), who, alongside his impressive career as international artist-architect, had joined the movement of the "Grass Mud Horse." Ai Wei Wei had started praising Chinese netizen culture and he himself contributed with provocations and commentaries about government policies. He also predicted that popular arts and netizen cultures would have their own ways of surviving, and would continue to stimulate the minds and hopes of Chinese citizens.

It became clear from our interviews that media industries and the related debates about sex culture are gradually expanding, despite the fact that web sites with sexual content are officially illegal and are indeed being regularly swept up in ongoing rounds of government imposed censorship (Wu et al. 2010). China is trying to perfect its immaculate infrastructure of highly-controlled Internet culture based on its vision of cosmopolitanism with uniquely Chinese characteristics (有中國特色的世界主義). Citizens are encouraged to be consumers of new fashions and lifestyles. At the same time, they are actively spied upon and reprimanded when pursuing politically-sensitive debates or circulating so-called vulgarities. While the Chinese government wants to generally support people's use of Internet culture, it also keeps it under a paranoid eye. Government agencies carry out unique forms of data mining and social networking to promote their Confucian-inspired policies, while netizens equally employ an ubiquitous gaze onto the life-styles and sexual choices of others (Lyon 2007). For instance, it is well known that the Chinese political police, the Ministry of Public Security (公安部), has recruited a vast network of intelligence agents within student communities to spy on Chinese citizens (Xiao 2010). Some netizens maintain a positive attitude, but others within the peer group are pushed to self-censor and are forced to conform to acceptable types of criticism. Often serving as double-agents of civic debate and government propaganda, netizens embody the era of internalized surveillance.

The excesses of Western sex and porn culture are routinely denounced by the Chinese government, but China itself has become one of the largest consumers of porn in the world and has enabled its own unique domains and platforms for user-generated content. Besides specifically locating a booming market along with an average citizen tolerance of sex industries, this book wishes to argue for a further rejuvenation of Chinese sex culture. Popular social networks such as Renren (人人网) have engendered creative expressivity and a playful DIY eroticism. Young people are optimistic, turned on and euphoric about seduction and online friendships, and are also willing to fight back to the larger control mechanisms of the nation-state.

The power of their erotic activism became more pronounced around the time of tightening government intrusion and surveillance in Spring 2010. Through daily news reports on web sites such as China Digital Times and China Media Project and micro-blogging networks such as Twitter, a large amount of reportage and informed opinion was made available to me on a daily basis. These platforms provided a wealth of information (along with English translations) concerning sensitive topics that could not have been shared in any other way.

As a result, the research blossomed and I began locating a more confident or optimistic point of view. It then became easier to search for Chinese role models and/or viral movements of culture that sought to take back control and embody or represent sexuality. For example, in recent years there have been notable trends of pornographic amateur videos that proudly feature local milieus and spaces. These videos often exhibit a juvenile and "naughty" imagination and create an atmosphere of sexual outburst – the idea that sex is happening spontaneously and everywhere and now people have found a way to meticulously document it. These DIY videos are also archived and shared in such a way that allows for categories of diverse Chinese provinces and cities, or specific spaces and places within cities, to be represented. These videos are less popular than the commercial products imported from Japan but they do provide a unique attempt at performance and sex education. One of my interviewees claimed that "it is very hard to get any information about sex acts in China and amateur pornography is the one way men try and learn about how to become better lovers."

An important part of this self-directed sex education is possibly to gain personal insights into how commercial pornography has hijacked the narratives of pleasure. Celebrity blogger Han Han (韓寒) sent an important message to Chinese youth when he officially recommended the work and personality of Japanese AV star Kaede Matsushima. While praising her personality, he added a postscript that one should not feel overly intimated by the phenomenal quality of her sex performances. Han Han struck the right note in defending the virtues of a porn star while deconstructing her make-believe or larger than life qualities.

Indeed, personal narratives of pleasure have to be reclaimed from manufactured superstars and the manipulated scripts of arousal and orgasm concocted by corporate industries. Thus, my analysis also includes the important work of well-known bloggers and sexperts such as Mu Zimei ((木子美) and Sister Swallow (流氓燕) who have paved the way in promoting a new sensibility around the Chinese sexual body and sex work. Sister Swallow is the long-term blogger who functions as a daily sexpert and who documents the daily struggles of sex workers in China. She candidly and amusingly informed me in an interview that she has little hope for academics to become allies and supportive partners in her defense of female pleasure and sex workers rights. While I agree with Sister Swallow that academic institutions are often unwilling to support grassroots initiatives on sexual pleasure, university students are actually very eager to have media discourses of sexuality on the curriculum.

Hence I tried to probe the expectations of the new generation and realized that their identities are indeed influence by global networks and joyful sexual attitudes. These young adults belong to a digital media generation weaned on micro-blogging as much as on older mass media, on new types of sexual celebrities besides those industries of "male-stream pornography." They are aware of the sex appeal of bloggers, amateur videos and underground celebrities. This also means that they are slowly growing accustomed to diversified tastes and are identifying with more fluid gender roles. Women are less interested than men in the dominant image of femininity as a skinny, youthful and submissive sex kitten.

The many student interviewees who volunteered to be interviewed for this book mostly belong to the sexualized 1980/1990s' generations and are knowledgeable about sexual diversity and the ins and outs of various sex industries. Some of the student groups were clearly female-dominated and were interested in debating gender and power dynamics in art, pornography and sex work. In our many interviews with young Chinese women about sexually explicit media, it became clear that they do not like simplistic or repetitive patriarchal constructions of femininity and sex. They are in need of more refined tastes and habits from those habituated by male-oriented commercial pornography.

Over the last decades, digital media networks have allowed women and queer groups to develop and distribute their own types of sexually explicit media and to create niche-industries (Jacobs 2007). For example, in Western Internet pornography there has been the genre BBW (Big Beautiful Women), where mature or overweight women present themselves as privileged objects of desire. Michael Goddard (2007) has shown that the genre of BBW thrives precisely because it makes up counter-mythologies to the more typical "vestigial anorexic artifacts" of commercial pornography. He argues that this Internet phenomenon typifies the non-normative potential of cyber culture, as it crosses boundaries between commercial and amateur porn and accommodates different ethnicities and media platforms that include blogs and dating sites for arranging personal affairs. All in all, the BBW phenomenon provides a novel space for the "volarization of excessive corporeality that would normatively be seen as monstrous" (Goddard 2007: 188). Goddard shows that this new idea of corporeality is not one of fixed fetishistic identity. Rather, BBW is a type of open-ended sensibility developed through the performance of diverging female and male roles.

My research into Chinese cybercultures equally shows that consumers are seeking to identify with a more open-ended sensibility about the body. They use the products available to them to question the worn-out gender roles inherent in commercial Japanese AV. Some Japanese AV movie genres have already caught up with this idea, even though these genres may be considered a marginal presence at this point. One such remarkable movie clip was forward to me by a fellow male-porn expert. I would like to describe it here so that readers can contemplate whether or not it could be a piquant novelty on the Chinese Internet. The movie excerpt shows two mature women who run a traditional Japanese hostel (ryokan) and are visited by a younger female friend who is a little bit younger and shy about sex. The movie opens very slowly and shows the hospitable and slightly worn-out faces of the mature women as they extensively prepare meals in the kitchen. But they do live as lovers and make time to spice up their sex life. At some point in the movie, after a kissing scene in the kitchen, they move to the futon mattress on the tatami floor. The camera zooms in on extensive licking, biting and fondling of breasts, and then offers ample (but pixilated) views of cunnilingus completed by a soundtrack of gasping and authentic-sounding orgasm. These sounds are vastly different from the average Japanese porn soundtrack, where young voices typically express a mixture of pleasure and fearful whimpering. In the second scene, one of the older women is taken a Japanese steam bath while the young visitor sits on the floor next to her, soaping and washing herself. The older women steps out of the bath to help her friend and begins to casually fondle her vagina. The twosome then put on their pajamas and move to the futon, where the young woman is slowly convinced to let herself go and experience a big orgasm.

Another Japanese movie that caught my attention for its differing feminine-spirited depiction of arousal and orgasm is Naho Ozawa's *Retirement – Going Back Home*, made by the famous porn star Naho Ozawa, produced in 2006 by the company KMP. The movie follows the commercial genre of "retirement video," which features porn stars in their mid-twenties or early thirties who decide to stop working as AV actresses or say farewell to a certain company. In this peculiar video, Ozawa travels back to the town that she grew up in and is interviewed while walking around its streets. She then invites several friends and porn stars to have a special intimate sex session with her. These sessions pay tribute to her body and emotive personality and her specific ways of reaching orgasm. Ozawa receives good, thorough sex from these multiple partners and she appears authentically moved and turned on. One of the sessions is so special and deep that it ends with her crying. In another scene, shot in what looks like somebody's private bedroom, the male lover's face is pixilated so it appears as if he is one of her ex-boyfriends meeting her at home. In yet another session, a bed is placed in the middle of the room and fans have been invited to join the session as spectators ringed around the bed. They are mostly quiet and respectful middle-aged men

Figure 1: Naho Ozawa's Retirement video – *Going Back Home*, made by the famous porn star Naho Ozawa, produced in 2006 by the company KMP.

who watch very carefully and then clap politely after the couple's orgasm. Because this movie as "retirement video" is designed and scripted to pay tribute to a sex goddess, it focuses on her sexual needs and talents and her ability to have and publicly-share deep orgasms.

At a first glance, it seems that my feminist interjections would be rejected by Chinese consumers. The recurring clichés of gender and power are taken for granted and still immensely popular amongst Chinese males. My speculation is that an open-ended sensibility and renovation of taste is underway and will be driven by a boom of newer genres, and female viewers who have confessed to be in need of sexually explicit media. There is still so much room for a positive female identification with sexually explicit media that may benefit from thought-provoking portrayals of gender and sexual orientations. These types of female-friendly or softer eroticism are currently rare products on the Chinese Internet but simply might be the next stage of porn cultural emancipation in China.[1]

It is also important, then, to think about the impact of sex and gender roles within Japanese ACG products. Hong Kong and Taiwan have, historically, been important trade routes and cultural crossroads for introducing new Japanese pop cultural products and subcultures into China. These products of Japanese and Korean ACG culture offer a safe platform for Chinese young adults to develop open-ended gender roles and express illicit fantasies. There is a unique type of temptation located in a projection of local desires and anxieties onto the exotic world of Japanese animation. As Anne Allison has argued, Japanese animation narratives are driven by a unique type of polymorphous perversity as they exhibit

> continual change and the stretching of desire across ever-new zones/bodies/products, and techno animism, the foregrounding of technology that animates spirits, creatures, and intimacies of various sorts. Resonant with the fluctuation, fragmentation, and speedup facing global youth across the world, such a fantasy also becomes addictive, compelling players to keep changing and expanding their play frontiers through a capitalism of endless innovation, information, and acquisition. (Allison 1996: 19)

And of course this ideal of fluctuating organisms is also presented in the genres of sexually explicit movies, which show a protagonist's overall disjointed quest for sexual gratification among a wide range of ghost-like entities. In the well-known hentai series, *La Blue Girl,* the girls are supernatural ninja's (literally: spies in disguise) who go around and seduce young men and have loud sex, while also getting visits from a perverted race of demons called the Shikima.[2] Protagonist Miko Mido is ruled by a tall and muscular demon-master Shikima Lord, also her father, who has inserted a small chip in her vagina. She is controlled by him but can utilize her "sexcraft" and carry out certain sex rituals to reverse his rule, which is ultimately how she will save the world from demons.

Chinese netizens and animation fans are defending local values and bodies as "sexcrafts" and yet are in constant dialogue with the pleasant waves of overseas products. In this way they can rejuvenate Chineseness while committing rebellion against the older patriarchial generations. It would be hoped that this movement would develop like a spider web, just like what happened with the obscenity debates and free speech movements in Japan. In *Adult Manga, Culture and Power in Contemporary Japanese Society,* Sharon Kinsella (2000) outlines the political uproar caused by soft-core and hardcore depictions in animation genres such as *Boy Love* and *Lolicon*. In many cases the movement against raunchy or sadistic scenes in animation was led by various anti-censorship proposals by government as well as citizen groups, such as housewives who were concerned about harmful and sexist content. Kinsella shows that the targeted genres survived by adopting means of self-regulation and by initiating a creative movement for freedom of expression. These campaigns for freedom gave manga artists a new potential to gain respectability, to network their painstaking efforts and to move their work into a more mainstream type of visibility (Kinsella 2000: 159.)

It has been shown that a Chinese art force and netizen culture is equally spreading its tentacles into the web. In opposition to nation-state methods of surveillance and humorless impotence, women have joined men in reclaiming and rewriting them as pearls of sex art and of eroticism.

Notes

1. Thanks to Florian Cramer and Gerrie Lim for sending me the Japanese AV which they thought I might like. I did like it and was happy that at least they could cater to a hybrid female and male gaze.
2. *La Blue Girl* is an erotic anime and manga series. Based on the manga by Toshio Maeda, the *La Blue Girl* anime, like his other hentai series features a large amount of tentacle rape. It departs somewhat from its predecessors, however, by lightening the atmosphere with humor, lightly parodying the "Tentacle Hentai" genre. An immensely successful series, *La Blue Girl* has inspired, over the years, several OVA series for a total of 14 episodes, a comic book adaptation, three live-action movies, some PC games, and some art-books.

References

Allison, Anne (2006) "The Japan Fad in Global Youth Culture and Millenial Capitalism," in Frenchy Lunning (ed) *Mechademia: Emerging Worlds of Anime and Manga*, Minneapolis: University of Minnesota Press.

Goddard, Michael (2007) "BBW: Techno-archaism, Excessive Corporeality and Network Sexuality," in Katrien Jacobs, Marije Janssen and Matteo Pasquinelli (eds) *Click Me, A Netporn Studies Reader,* Amsterdam: Institute of Network Cultures.

Ho, Sik-Ying and Tsang, K.T. (2006) "The Things Girls Shouldn't See: Relocating The Penis in Sex Education in Hong Kong," *Sex Education* 2: 1, pp. 61–73.

Jacobs, Katrien (2007) *Netporn: DIY Web Culture and Sexual Politics,* Maryland: Rowman and Littlefield.

Kinsella, Sharon (2000) *Adult Manga: Culture and Power in Contemporary Japanese Society,* Honolulu: ConsumAsiaN, Curzon Press and the University of Hawaii.

UNIVERSITY OF WINCHESTER LIBRARY

Lyon, David (2007) *Surveillance Studies: An Overview*, Malden MA: Polity Press.

South China Morning Post (CMP) (2010) "Falstaffian Spirit is Missing on Mainland," 6 September.

Wu, Zhaohui et al., (2010) "A Peep at Pornography Web In China," *Websci'10*, 27 April, North Carolina, USA http://journal.webscience.org/306 (accessed 12 July 2011).

Xiao, Qiang (2010) "DSD Police Recruit and Maintain Informant Networks Among University Students," 11 April, http://chinadigitaltimes.net/2010/04/dsd-police-recruit-and-maintain-informant-networks-among-university-students/ (accessed 12 July 2011).

Bibliography

Agence France-Press (2010) "Pop Star Detained in Indonesia's first celebrity sex video scandal," *South China Morning Post,* 23 June.

Ai Wei Wei Blog Excerpt (2009) in Zhai Minglei, Zhong Guo Meng Bo and Chan Wun Ying (eds) *China's Fierce Bloggers, The Power of Civil Discourses in the Age of New Media.* Hong Kong, Tiandi Book, September, pp. 43–47.

Allison, Anne (2006) "The Japan Fad in Global Youth Culture and Millenial Capitalism," in Frenchy Lunning (ed) *Mechademia: Emerging Worlds of Anime and Manga,* Minneapolis: University of Minnesota Press.

Anderson, Nate (2010) "Sociologists invade World of Warcraft," 11 May, http://arstechnica.com/tech-policy/news/2010/05/sociologists-invade-world-of-warcraft-and-see-humanitys-future.ars

Arnold, Emily and Bailey, Marlon (2009) "Constructing Home and Family: How the Ballroom Community Supports African American GLBTQ Youth in the Face of HIV/ AIDS," *Journal of Gay & Lesbian Social Services,* 21: 2, pp. 171–88.

Bandurski, David (2011) "Global Times Attacks Ai Wei Wei and the West," Posted for *China Media Project.* Available at http://cmp.hku.hk/2011/04/07/11340/ (accessed 7 May 2011).

Bergner, Daniel (2009) "What do Women Want?," *The New York Times* (online), 22 January, http://www.nytimes.com/2009/01/25/magazine/25desire-t.html (accessed 18 May 2011).

Bernstein, Elizabeth (2007) *Temporarily Yours: Intimacy, Authenticity, and the Commerce of Sex,* Chicago: University of Chicago Press.

BBC News (2010) "Pornography Virus Published Web History of Victims On Net," *BBC News* (online), 15 April, http://news.bbc.co.uk/2/hi/8622665.stm (accessed 29 July 2011).

Boyd, Danah (2007) "Viewing American Class Divisions through Facebook and MySpace," *Danah Boyd Blog,* 24 June, Available at http://www.danah.org/papers/essays/Classdivisions.html (accessed 2 October, 2009).

Braidotti, Rosi (2005) "A Critical Cartography of Feminist Post-Postmodernism," *Australian Feminist Studies,* 20: 47, pp.169–79.

Bright, Susie (2005) "Nerve Lovers' Uproar." *Susie Bright Blog,* 19 September, http://susiebright.blogs.com/susie_brights_journal_/2005/09/nerve_lovers_in.html (accessed 15 July, 2010).

Burns, Simon (2006) "Nude bloggers upset China beauty contest," *V3.co.uk,* 25 May. http://www.v3.co.uk/vnunet/news/2156937/china-bloggers-beauty-contest (accessed 19 July 2011).

Chang, Ying (2009) "State Broadcast Television Administration Recalled Wo Ju for a Second Trial. The 2.0 Version Shall Be A Purified One," *Xinhuanet,* 1 December, http://www.tj.xinhuanet.com/movieteleplay/2009-12/01/content_18377113.htm (accessed 11 July 2011).

Cheng, Jacqui (2008) "20% of Teens Say They've Put Nude Pics of Themselves Online," *Ars Technica,* 19 September, http://arstechnica.com/news.ars/post/20081211-20-of-teens-say-theyve-put-nude-pics-of-themselves-online.html (accessed 12 July 2011).

Chien, Eugenia (2005) "China's Sexual Blogolution," posted on *Alternet.org*, 12 Nov, http://www.alternet.org/story/28145/china%27s_sexual_blogolution

China Digital Times (2009) "China Says 5395 arrested in Pornography Crackdown," *China Digital Times* (online) 31 December, http://chinadigitaltimes.net/2009/12/china-says-5394-arrested-in-Internet-pornography-crackdown/ (accessed 11 July 2011).

Chivers, Meredith, Rieger, Gerulf, Latty, Elizabeth and Bailey, Michael (2004) "A Sex Difference in the Specificity of Sexual Arousal," *Psychological Science*, 4: 11 pp. 736–44.

Chun, Wendy (2006) *Control and Freedom: Power and Paranoia in The Age of Fiber optics*, Cambridge, MA: MIT Press.

CNN.com (2010) "China's Rebel Blogger," 4 June, http://edition.cnn.com/2010/TECH/web/06/03/han.han.china/index.html (accessed 8 July 2011).

Cody, Edward (2005) "In Chinese Cyberspace, a Blossoming Passion," *The Washington Post* (online), 19 July. http://www.washingtonpost.com/wp-dyn/content/article/2005/07/18/AR2005071801561.html (accessed 19 July 2011).

Demick, Barbara (2010) "Paranoia the Best Censor," *South China Morning Post,* 24 April.

Doane, Mary Anne (1991) *Femmes Fatales: Feminism, Film Theory, and Psychoanalysis,* New York: Routledge.

Donath, Judith and Boyd, D. (2004) "Public Displays of Connections," *BT Technology Journal*, 22: 4, pp. 71–82.

Ellison, Nicole, Heino, R. and Gibbs, J. (2006) "Managing Impressions Online: Self-Presentations Processes in the Online Dating Environment," *Journal of Computer-Mediated Communication*, 11: 2, pp. 1–24.

Farrer, James (2007) "China's Women Sex Bloggers and Dialogic Sexual Politics on the Chinese Internet," *China Aktuell*, 36: 4, pp. 9–45.

February Girl (2006) "Exposed? Immoral? Get undressed!" 1 March, http://blog.sina.com.cn/s/blog_48c22252010002se.html This blog post was translated into English on *EastSouthWestNorth* blog http://www.zonaeuropa.com/20060312_1.htm, March 2006 (accessed 15 July 2011).

Fei, Na (2010) 我从不妄自菲薄--专访日本女优苍井空 wo cong bu wang zi fei bo – zhuan fang ri ben nv you cang jing kong (I never look down upon myself – Interview with Japanese actress Sola Aoi), *Nanfang Weekend* (online), June 23. http://www.infzm.com/content/46724 (accessed 11 July 2011).

Feng, Chien-san (2009) "Between Alternative and Mainstream, Independence and Nationhood," in Lam Oi-Wan and Ip Iam-Chong (eds) *Info Rhizome: report on independent media in the Chinese-speaking world*, Hong Kong: In-Media.

Foucault, Michel (1990) *A History of Sexuality, Vol. 1: And Introduction,* London: Vintage.

Gilmore, Anthony (2010) "China's New Gold Farm," in *Virtual World Research*, 2: 4, https: //journals.tdl.org/jvwr/article/view/863/628 (accessed 13 July 2011).

Goddard, Michael (2007) "BBW: Techno-archaism, Excessive Corporeality and Network Sexuality," in Katrien Jacobs, Marije Janssen and Matteo Pasquinelli (eds) *Click Me, A Netporn Studies Reader,* Amsterdam: Institute of Network Cultures.

Golub, Alex and Lingley, Kate (2008) "Just Like the Qing Empire: Internet addiction, MMOGs, and moral crisis in Contemporary China," in *Games and Culture*, 3: 1, pp. 59–75.

Gustines, George Gene (2010)"Out of the Closet and Up, Up and Away," *The New York Times*, 16 April.

Han Han (2009) Blog Excerpt, in Zhai Minglei, Zhong Guo Meng Bo and Chan Wun Ying (eds), *China's Fierce Bloggers, The Power of Civil Discourses in the Age of New Media*, Hong Kong, Tiandi Book, (pp. 73–99). Han Han's blog is located at http://blog.sina.com.cn/twocold (accessed 11 July 2011).

Han Han (2010a) "Google in China, *China Digital Times* (online), 15 January, translated by Anne Anna, http://chinadigitaltimes.net/2010/01/han-han-speaks-out-on-google-in-china/ (accessed 11 July 2011).

Han Han (2010b) "From Now On, I am a Vulgar Person." *China Digital Times* (online) 22 January, Translated by China Geeks. http://chinadigitaltimes.net/2010/01/han-han-%E2%80%9Cfrom-now-on-i%E2%80%99m-a-vulgar-person%E2%80%9D/ (accessed 15 May 2010).

He, Qinglian (2008) *The Fog of Censorship: Media Control in China*, New York: Human Rights in China.

Henan People Daily (2009) "China Youth Daily: Zhoukou City Serves and Guides the Youth in Creating a New Internet Space, 30 November, http://henan.people.com.cn/news/2009/11/30/437919.html Translated on *China Digital Times* http://chinadigitaltimes.net/china/Internet-commentators (accessed 11 July 2011).

Ho, Sik-Ying and Tsang, K.T. (2006) "The Things Girls Shouldn't See: Relocating The Penis in Sex Education in Hong Kong," *Sex Education* 2: 1, pp. 61–73.

Holmes, Brian (2008) "One World, One Dream: China at the Risk of New Subjectivities," 8 January, http://brianholmes.wordpress.com/2008/01/08/one-world-one-dream/ (accessed 11 July 2011).

Hopkins, Jim (2007) "Penthouse makes $500M hookup with Social Site Various," *USA Today* (online), 12 December. Available at http://www.usatoday.com/tech/techinvestor/corporatenews/2007-12-12-penthouse_N.htm (accessed 13 July 2011).

Hu, Yong (2009) "Why Remain Independent and How to Be Alternative?" in Lam Oiwan and Ip Iam-Chong (eds) *Info Rhizome: report on independent media in the Chinese-speaking world*, Hong Kong: In-Media.

Iwabuchi, Koichi (2002) *Recentering Globalization: Popular Culture and Japanese Transnationalism*, Durham: Duke University Press.

Jacobs, Andrew (2010) "Heartthrob's Blog Challenges China's Leaders," *New York Times* (online), 12 March, http://www.nytimes.com/2010/03/13/world/asia/13Han Han.html (accessed 11 July 2011).

Jacobs, Katrien, *Netporn: DIY Web Culture and Sexual Politics* Lanham MD: Rowman and Littlefield, 2007.

Janssen, Erick, Carpenter, Deanna and Graham, Cynthia A. (2003) "Selecting Films for Sex Research: Gender Differences in Erotic Film Preference," *Archives of Sexual Behavior*, 32: 3 pp. 243–51.

Jiang, Liuqiao (2010) 安徽一贪官被曝与500女性有染 妻子发现 "性爱日记" an hui yi tan guan bei bao yu 500 nv xing you ran, qi zi fa xian xing ai ri ji. (A corrupted officer was caught having affairs with 500 women. The wife found the "Sex Diary."), *Anhuinews.com* (online), 7 April, http://politics.people.com.cn/GB/14562/11307497.html (accessed 11 July 2011).

Jingbao (2001) "Porn invades students' pockets" Seqing duwu ruqin xuesheng koudai (色情读物 "入侵" 学生口袋,) in *Jingbao* (晶报), Shenzhensheqing (深圳社情), Shenzhen, 8 November.

Jones, Gary (2007) "The Blogger Who Took on China," 12 February, http://www.thefirstpost.co.uk/2231,news-comment,news-politics,the-blogger-who-took-on-china (accessed 11 July 2011).

Kelsky, Karen (2001) *Women on the Verge: Japanese Women, Western Dreams*, Durham: Duke University Press.

Kinsella, Sharon (2000) *Adult Manga: Culture and Power in Contemporary Japanese Society*, Honolulu: ConsumAsiaN, Curzon Press and the University of Hawaii.

Kipnis, Laura (1996) *Bound and Gagged: Pornography and the Politics of Fantasy in America*, New York: Grove.

Lam, Bourree (2009) "Money Shots: A Look at the Hong Kong Porn Industry," *Time Out Hong Kong*, 13 October, http://www.timeout.com.hk/feature-stories/features/28969/money-shots-a-look-at-the-hong-kong-porn-industry.html (accessed 11 July 2011).

Lam, Oiwan (2007) "Don't Turn Hong Kong into a Mono-Colour Ghost City," Interview with Oiwan Lam, *Interlocals* (online) 2 July. http://interlocals.net/?q=node/118 (accessed 11 July 2011).

Lam, Oiwan (2009a) "Declaration of Anonymous Netizens," *Global Voices Online* (online), 24 June, http://advocacy.globalvoicesonline.org/2009/06/24/china-2009-declaration-of-the-anonymous-netizens (accessed 17 July 2011).

Lam, Oiwan (2009b) "Good Bye Grass Mud Horse," *Global Voices Online*, 18 March, http://globalvoicesonline.org/2009/03/18/china-goodbye-grass-mud-horse/ (accessed 13 July 2011).

Lam, Oi-Wan and Ip Iam-Chong (eds) (2009) *Info Rhizome: report on independent media in the Chinese-speaking world*, Hong Kong: Hong Kong In-Media.

Landay, Lori (2010) "Rethinking Virtual Commodification, or The Virtual Kitchen Sink," *Virtual World Research*, 2: 4 (online), https: //journals.tdl.org/jvwr/article/view/860/625 (accessed 11 July 2011).

Lehman, Peter (2007) "You and Voyeurweb: Illustrating the Shifting Representation of the Penis on Internet with User-Generated Content," *Cinema Journal* 46: 4, pp. 105–15.

Leung, Isaac (nd)"The Impossibility of Having Sex with 500 Men in a Month-I'm an Oriental Whore" Information available at http://isaacleung.com/orientalwhore/ (no longer available) Liz Hao (2011) "College Girls Promotes Nude Art," *Shenzhen Daily* (online), 4 March, http://www.szdaily.com/content/2011-03/04/content_5396842.htm (accessed 11 July 2011).

Li, Yinhe (2010) Video interview about Swinging Professor Ma, *Joy.cn*, 21 May, http://news.joy.cn/2010/njjzyl/ (accessed 11 July 2011).

Lian, Yue (2009) Blog Excerpt, "Cross the River By Feeling Nipples," in Zhai Minglei, Zhong Guo Meng Bo and Chan Wun Ying (eds) *China's Fierce Bloggers, The Power of Civil Discourses in the Age of New Media,* Hong Kong, Tiandi Book (pp. 41).

Lim, Gerrie (2004) *Invisible Trade: High-Class Sex for Sale in Singapore*, Singapore: Monsoon Books.

Lim, Gerrie (2007) "The State of Asian Pornography," In *Asian Sex Gazette* (online) 1 July, originally published in AVN.online.com and reprinted with permission, http://www.asiansexgazette.com/asg/southeast_asia/southeast08news76.htm (accessed 11 July, 2011).

Liu, Tina (2009) "Conflicting Discourses on Boys' Love and Subcultural Tactics in Mainland China and Hong Kong," in Mark McLelland and Fran Martin (eds) *Intersections: Gender and Sexuality in Asia and the Pacific* http://intersections.anu.edu.au/issue20/liu.htm (accessed 11 July 2011).

Livingston, Jennie (1991) *Paris is Burning* (DVD) Off White, Miramax.

Luo, Yanghuo (2009) Blog Excerpt, in Zhai Minglei, Zhong Guo Meng Bo and Chan Wun Ying (eds) *China's Fierce Bloggers, The Power of Civil Discourses in the Age of New Media* . Hong Kong, Tiandi Book (pp. 232–38).

Lyon, David (2007) *Surveillance Studies: An Overview*, Malden MA: Polity Press.

Mackie, Vera (2009) "Transnational Bricolage: Gothic Lolita and the Political Economy of Fashion," In Mark McLelland and Fran Martins (eds) *Intersections: Gender and Sexuality in Asia and the Pacific,* 20April http://intersections.anu.edu.au/issue20/mackie.htm (accessed 11 July 2011).

MacKinnon, Rebeca (2009) "Independent Media in the Chinese-speaking world," in Lam Oiwan and Ip Iam-Chong (eds) *Info Rhizome: report on independent media in the Chinese-speaking world,* Hong Kong: In-Media.

Mackinnon, Rebecca (2010) "Chinese Netizens Open Letter to the Chinese Government and Google," *R Conversation Blog* (online), 21March, http://rconversation.blogs.com/rconversation/2010/03/chinese-netizens-open-letter-to-the-chinese-government-and-google.html (accessed 13 July 2011).

McBeth, John (2010) "Moral Outrage Smacks of Hypocrisy," *The Straits Times*, 26 June.

McKenna, Katelyn (2006) "A Progressive Affair: Online Dating to Real World Mating," in Monica T. Witty, Andrea J. Baker and James A. Inman (eds), *Online matchmaking*, New York: Palgrave (pp. 116–36).

McLelland, Mark (2000) "No Climax, No Point, No Meaning? Japanese Women's Boy-Love Sites on the Internet," *Journal of Commercial Inquiry*, 24: 3, pp. 52–69.

McLelland, Mark (2009) "(A)cute Confusion: The Unpredictable Journey of Japanese Popular Culture," in Mark McLelland and Fran Martin (eds) *Intersections: Gender and Sexuality in Asia and the Pacific*, 20 April, http://intersections.anu.edu.au/issue20/mclelland.htm (accessed 29 July 2011).

Madargia, Julen (2010) "Charter 08: Why it should be called Wang," *ChinaYouRen Blog*, 1 January, http://chinayouren.com/en/2009/01/11/1101 (accessed 13 July 2011).

Marchetti, Gina (1993) *Romance and the Yellow Peril: Race, Sex and Discursive Strategies in Hollywood Fiction*, Berkeley and LA: University of California Press.

Merewether, Charles (2008) "Ruins in Reverse," *Ai Weiwei: Under Construction*, catalogue, Sydney: New South Wales Press.

Ming Pao (2007) "Hong Kong Book Fair to Sell Pornographic Comics," *Ming Pao Daily* (online) 24 July (no longer available).

Mizoguchi, Akiko (2010) "Towards Activism of Pleasure: Possibilities of Yaoi as a Productive Queer Forum," paper, *ACS Crossroads* conference, Lingnan University, Hong Kong, June.

Mowlabocus, Sharif (2010) "Porn 2.0? Technology, Social Practice, and the New Online Porn Industry," in Feona Attwod (ed) *Porn.com. Making Sense of Online Pornography*, New York: Peter Lang (pp. 69–88).

Nakamura, Lisa (2002) *Cybertypes: Race, Ethnicity, and Identity on the Internet*, New York: Routledge.

Nardi, Bonnie (2010) *My Life as Night Elf Priest*, Ann Arbor: University of Michigan Press.

Ng, Man Lune (2006) "Hong Kong. The International Encyclopedia of Sexuality at Humboldt University," http://www2.hu-berlin.de/sexology/IES/hongkong.html (accessed 12 July 2011).

Nip, Amy (2010) "Censors delete 95pc of Blogs a Day, Forum Told," *South China Morning Post*, 20 June.

Orbaugh, Sharalyn (2003) "Busty Battlin' Babes: the Evolution of the Shojo in 1990s Visual Culture," Norman Bryson, Maribeth Graybill, and Joshua Mostow (eds) *Gender and Power in the Japanese Visual Field*, Honolulu: Hawaii University Press (pp. 200–28).

Ottomo, Massimo (2010) "A Field Guide to Sola Aoi, The Pornography Star who Brought Down China's Great Firewall," 22 April, http://fleshbot.com/5522012/a-field-guide-to-sola-aoi-the-pornographystar-who-brought-down-chinas-great-firewall (accessed 13 May 2010).

Parish, William L., Lauman, Edward O. and Mojola, Sanyu A. (2007) 'Sexual Behavior in China: Trends and Comparisons," *Population and Development Review*, 33: 4, pp. 729–56.

Pasquinelli, Matteo (2009) *Animal Spirits: A Bestiary of the Commons*, Rotterdam: Nai Publishers.

Pearlman, Ellen (2009) "Chinese Women: Sexuality and Costume as Power and Individuation," Paper presented at Conference, *Extra/Ordinary Dresscode: Costuming and the Second Skin in Asia*, City University of Hong Kong, November.

Pei Yuxin, Ho Sik-Ying and Man Lun Ng (2007) "Studies on Women's Sexuality in China since 1980: A Critical Review," *Journal of Sex Research*, 2007, 44: 2, pp. 202–12.

Pei, Yuxin and Ho Sik-Ying (2009) "Gender, Self and Pleasure; Young Women's Discourses on Masturbation in Contemporary Shanghai," *Culture, Health, and Sexuality*, 1: 5, pp. 515–28.

Plummer, Ken (1995) *Telling Sexual Stories: Power, Change, and Social Worlds*, New York and London: Routledge.

Quartly, James (2010) "Believe in Sister Phoenix. It only took 100 years," *China Daily* (online), 10 March, http://www.chinadaily.com.cn/life/2010-03/10/content_9566092.htm (accessed 11 July 2011).

Reed-Danahay, Deborah (ed) 1997*Auto/Ethnography: Rewriting the Self and the Social,* UK Oxford: Berg.

Rofel, Lisa (2007) *Desiring China: Experiments in Neoliberalism, Sexuality, and Public Culture,* Durham: Duke University Press.

Saito, Tamaki (2007) "Otaku Sexuality," in Christopher Bolton, Istvan Csicsery-Ronay Jr and Takyuki Tatsumi (eds) *Robot Ghosts and Wired Dreams. Japanese Science Fictions from Origins to Anime,* Minneapolis: University of Minnesota Press (pp. 222–50).

Sampson, Tony (2009) "How Networks Become Viral," in *The Spambook: On Viruses, Pornography, and Other Anomalies from the Dark Side of Digital Culture* New Jersey: Hampton Press (pp. 39–61).

Schokora, Adam J. (2008) "China's first blogger on the Chinese blogosphere," *Danwei.org,* 6 August, http://www.danwei.org/Internet/isaac_mao_and_the_chinese_blog.php (accessed 11 July 2011).

Schokora, Adam J. (2009) "Ai Wei Wei Naked," *56 Minus One Blog,* 2 June, http://56minus1.com/2009/05/ai-weiwei-naked (accessed 11 July 2011).

Sheller, Mimi (2007) "Virtual Islands: Mobilities, Connectivity, and the New Caribbean Spatialities," *Small Axe* 24, October, pp. 16–33.

Shi, Jingtao (2011) "Ai Wei Wei Accused of Huge Tax Scam," *South China Morning Post*, 21 May.

South China Morning Post, "1,332 Guilty of Spreading Porn," 6 November 2010.

Siuming, Pan (2006) "Transformations in the Primary Life Cycle: the Origins and Nature of China's Sexual Revolution," in E. Jeffreys (ed) *Sex and Sexuality in China,* New York: Routledge,

Skirmisher (2007) "Living in a Glass House: China's Version," Posted on *Skirmisher.org,* 16 May, http://skirmisher.org/culture/living-in-a-glass-house-chinas-version (accessed 8 July 2011).

Smith, Clarissa (2007) *One for the Girls: The Pleasures and Practices of Reading Women's Porn,* Bristol, UK: Intellect.

South China Morning Post (SCMP) (2010) 'Falstaffian Spirit is Missing on Mainland,' 6 September.

South China Morning Post (SCMP) (2010) "1,332 Guilty of Spreading Porn," 6 November.

Stuttgen, Tim (ed) (2010) *Post/Porn/Politics: Queer_Feminist Perspcetive on the Politics andof Porn Performance and Sex_Work as Cultural Production,* Berlin: B_books.

Tancer, Bill (2007) "Facebook: More popular Than Porn," *Time Magazine* (online), 31 October, http://www.time.com/time/business/article/0,8599,1678586,00.html (accessed 13 July 2011)

Taylor, Lucien (ed) (1994) *Visualizing Theory: Selected Essay from V.A.R 1990-1994,* London: Routledge.

Thaemlitz,Terre (2008) "Viva McGlam: Is Transgenderism a Critique of or Capitulation to Opulence-Driven Glamour Models?" http://www.comatonse.com/writings/vivamcglam.html (accessed July 10, 2011).

The Telegraph (2008) "Chinabounder Sex Blogger Reveals His Identity", *Telegraph.co.uk* (online) 17 July.

Tiger Temple (2009) Blog Excerpt, in Zhai Minglei, Zhong Guo Meng Bo and Chan Wun Ying (eds), *China's Fierce Bloggers, The Power of Civil Discourses in the Age of New Media,* Hong Kong, Tiandi Book (pp. 147–71).

Times of India (2009) "China Pays Surfers To Find Pornography," *The Times of India* (online), 7 December, http://chinadigitaltimes.net/2009/12/china-pays-web-surfers-to-find-porn/ (accessed 11 July 2011).

Wang, Tricia (2010) "Googlist Realism: the Google-China Saga Posits Free-Information Regimes as a New Site of Cultural imperialism and Moral Tensions," *CulturalBytes.com*, July 10, http://culturalbytes.com/post/7818762.73/googoochinasaga (accessed 11 July 2011).

Wilde, Jonathan (2005) "The Emancipation of Mumu," *Distributed Republic Blog* (online) 30 November, http://www.distributedrepublic.net/archives/2005/11/30/the-emancipation-of-mu-mu (accessed 11 July 2011).

Williams, Sue (1997) *China: A Century of Revolution.* Zeitgeist Films, Information available at http://www.zeitgeistfilms.com/film.php?directoryname=chinaacenturyofrevolution (accessed 11 July 2011).

Wong, Edward (2010) "18 Orgies Later, Chinese Swinger Gets Prison Bed," *New York Times* (online), 20 May. http://www.nytimes.com/2010/05/21/world/asia/21china.html (accessed 17 July 2010).

Wong, Nicole (2009) "Getting Noticed at Last" *China Daily* (online) 24 January, http://www.chinadaily.com.cn/hkedition/2009-01/24/content_7426638.htm (accessed 11 July 2011).

Wong, Wendy Siuyi (2006) "Globalizing Manga: From Japan to Hong Kong and Beyond," in Lunning Frenchy (ed) *Mechademia 1: Emerging Worlds of Anime and Manga* (pp.23–45).

Wu, Zhaohui et al. (2010) "A Peep at Pornography Web In China," in *Proceedings of the WebSci10: Extending the Frontiers of Society On-Line*, 26-27th April, Raleigh, NC: US. http://journal.webscience.org/306 (accessed 11 May 2011).

Xiao, Qang (2010) "Han Han Person of the Year and his New Magazine," *China Digital Times* (online) 10 January, http://chinadigitaltimes.net/2010/01/han-han-%E9%9F%A9%E5%AF%92-person-of-the-year-2009-and-his-new-magazine/ (accessed 15 July 2011).

Xiao, Qiang (2010) "DSD Police Recruit and Maintain Informant Networks Among University Students," 11 April, http://chinadigitaltimes.net/2010/04/dsd-police-recruit-and-maintain-informant-networks-among-university-students/ (accessed 12 July 2011)

Xie, Qingyun (2010) "China's Anti-Pornography Campaign Starts Green Bookmark Action 2010," *Sing Tao Global Network* (online) 13 June, http://feature.stnn.cc/news/saohuang/ (accessed 11 July 2011).

Xinhua Agency (2010) "China Issues White Paper on Internet Policy," 8 June, http://china.org.cn/china/2010-06/08/content_20206978_3.htm (accessed 11 July 2011).

Xu, Yong and Yu Na (2009) *Solution Scheme*, Hong Kong: Culture of China Publication Co.

Xue Ying (2009) "Green Dam: Chinese Netizens are All Children," *Cn Reviews* (online)16 June, http://cnreviews.com/life/news-issues/green-dam-chinese-neitzens-children_20090616.html (accessed 11 July 2011).

Yang, Guobin (2010) "Why Google Should Not Quit," *Social Science Research Council Website* (online), 15 January, http://www.ssrc.org/features/view/why-google-should-not-quit (accessed 11 July 2011).

Yang Guobin (2009) *The Power of the Internet in China: Citizens Activism Online*, New York: Columbia University Press.

Yau, Ching (2010) "Porn Power: Sexual and Gender Politics in Li Han-hsiang's *Fengyue* Films," in Yau Ching (ed) *As Normal as Possible: Negotiating Sexuality and Gender in Mainland China and Hong Kong*, Hong Kong University Press.

Yau, H.Y. and Wong, H.W. (2009) "The Emergence of a New Sexual Ideal: A Case Study of Yuki Maiko's Pornographic VCDs in Hong Kong", *Journal of Archaeology and Anthropology*, 70 (2009), pp. 1–46.

Yu, Verna (2010) "Chopping Away At the Wall of Injustice," *South China Morning Post,* 5 April.

Zakari, Chantal (nd) *webAffairs,* http://www.webaffairsbook.info/webAffairs1.html (accessed 11 July 2011).

Zhai, Minglei (2009) Blog Excerpt, in Zhai Minglei, Zhong Guo Meng Bo and Chan Wun Ying (eds), *China's Fierce Bloggers, The Power of Civil Discourses in the Age of New Media* (p. 483), Hong

Kong: Tiandi Book. Zhang Minglei's blogs are located at www.1bao.org, http://www.bulloger.com/blogs/1bao (accessed 16 June 2010).

Zhai, Minglei, Zhong Guo Meng Bo and Chan Wun Ying (eds) (2009) *China's Fierce Bloggers, The Power of Civil Discourses in the Age of New Media*, Hong Kong: Tiandi Book.

Zhang, Lifan (2010) "A Confession of an Internet Naked Runner," Translated by Oiwan Lam, In *Global Voices Online*, 5 March, http://globalvoicesonline.org/2010/03/05/china-a-confession-of-an-Internet-naked-runner/ (accessed 11 July 2011).

Zheng, Tiantian (2009) *Red Lights: The Lives of Sex Workers in Postsocialist China*, Minneapolis: University of Minnesota Press.

Index